REAL LIFE LORE PRESENTS

Answers to Questions You've Never Asked

Cover Design: Roberto Nuñez
Layout Design: Elina Diaz
Writing contributions by Gary M. Krebs, GMK Writing and Editing, Inc.

For permission requests, please contact the publisher at:

Mango Publishing Group
2850 Douglas Road, 3rd Floor
Coral Gables, FL 33134 USA
Info@mango.bz

For special orders, quantity sales, course adoptions and corporate sales, please email the publisher at sales@mango.bz. For trade and wholesale sales, please contact Ingram Publisher Services at customer.service@ingramcontent.com or +1.800.509.4887.

Answers to Questions You've Never Asked: Explaining the "What If" in Science, Geography, and the Absurd

Library of Congress Cataloging
ISBN: (Paperback) 978-1-63353-935-8, (hardcover) 978-1-63353-669-2, (ebook) 978-1-63353-670-8
Library of Congress Control Number: 2017956261
BISAC category code : REF018000, REFERENCE/Questions & Answers

Printed in the United States of America

REAL LIFE LORE PRESENTS

Answers to Questions You've Never Asked

EXPLAINING THE "WHAT IF" IN SCIENCE, GEOGRAPHY, AND THE ABSURD

Joseph Pisenti

CORAL GABLES

*To my parents and professors—for inspiring creativity
and nurturing it through life.*

No one is dumb who is curious. The people who don't ask questions remain clueless throughout their lives.

—Neil deGrasse Tyson, astrophysicist

CONTENTS

INTRODUCTION: WHO AM I AND WHY DOES THIS BOOK EXIST?   9

CHAPTER ONE WHY DO STRANGE BORDERS EXIST?   13

CHAPTER TWO WHAT IF HISTORICAL EMPIRES WERE TO REUNITE TODAY?   23

CHAPTER THREE HOW FAR AWAY CAN YOU GET FROM CERTAIN THINGS?   47

CHAPTER FOUR HOW MANY COUNTRIES ARE THERE IN THE WORLD—
NOBODY KNOWS!   59

CHAPTER FIVE A TUTORIAL ON CREATING YOUR OWN COUNTRY   83

CHAPTER SIX PRESIDENTS, POLITICS, AND THE NUCLEAR FOOTBALL   97

CHAPTER SEVEN WHY IS MONEY BACKED BY GOLD?   105

CHAPTER EIGHT WHAT IS CREDIT AND WHERE DID IT COME FROM?   117

CHAPTER NINE WHAT IS THE MOST DANGEROUS ROAD IN THE WORLD?   127

CHAPTER TEN CAN YOU TURN THE EARTH INTO A SANDWICH?   137

CHAPTER ELEVEN THE LEAST YOU NEED TO KNOW ABOUT
EVERY US PRESIDENT   147

CONCLUSION MISCELLANEOUS THOUGHTS AND FACTS   195

TRIVIA ANSWERS   203

NOTES   211

AUTHOR   213

INTRODUCTION:
WHO AM I AND WHY DOES THIS BOOK EXIST?

Real knowledge is to know the extent of one's ignorance.

—Confucius

I've always been a huge fan of maps, geography, statistics, and economics. That may sound boring to some of you, but I've always found these subjects to be endlessly fascinating.

Ever since I was a little kid I loved playing strategy games like Axis & Allies, Risk, Settlers of Catan and video games like *Civilization IV*, *Age of Empires*, *Total War*, and *Europa Universalis/Crusader Kings*. These games all had beautiful maps and flavor that have inspired the way I create videos and think about the world.

I attribute my early fascination with strategy games to why I'm so attracted to strange questions today. I would play these games and try to recreate historical empires or kingdoms, and I basically do that now for YouTube videos instead of just for my own personal enjoyment. I love sharing the thoughts running through my head with so many people.

The Lore Behind *RealLifeLore*

RealLifeLore came into being during my final semester as a college undergraduate. It was February 2016, and I decided to create a unique channel as an outlet for my passion projects.

I faced many trials starting out. I remember being convinced early on that my videos would go viral overnight—only to wake up and see that they only had one hundred views. I had many naysayers among my family and friends who argued that YouTube was too saturated for any new channel to become popular.

At the same time, I was encouraged by the positive reviewer comments I received and continued undaunted. I'm glad I kept trying. Too often people start a project and get discouraged without even giving it enough of a chance to succeed. Within just a relatively brief amount of time, my *RealLifeLore* videos ultimately did go viral and today they receive millions of page views. I genuinely appreciate the kudos, criticisms, and suggestions from the viewers; I take all of these comments quite seriously and do my best do deliver the facts on what you want to learn about.

Of course, there are those comments that surprise me. The most common request I receive is to reveal my face. I find this surprising because I believe that seeing a narrator's face sometimes ruins the production. When you read a book, for example, you create the faces of all the characters in your head. You create this mental image of a person. When a fictional work is adapted as a film or TV show, your perceptions of those characters are shattered. For this reason, I'd prefer not to pull back the curtain and reveal the face behind *RealLifeLore*. I'm afraid you'll have to just use your imagination and suffer in suspense. (I'll give you this hint: I don't look as good as Chris Hemsworth nor do I have any noteworthy disfigurements.)

In a nutshell, this is how I view *RealLifeLore*: It is a popular YouTube video channel all about asking and answering questions you may never have thought about. The videos pose questions on little-known areas of geography, economics, and science, such as: *what if everyone lived in the same city? how deep is the ocean? and how big do tsunamis really get?*

If you haven't deduced it already, *size* and *proportion* really do matter when it comes to *RealLifeLore*. If the video channel has a core philosophy, it's to encourage people to *think differently and critically*. (All right, I concede the first part sounds a bit Steve Jobsian.) I pose challenging questions that many people have never considered. We learn when we ask ourselves questions we can't answer. Learning comes from seeking out the answers to unknown things. I believe that it's a fundamental part of human nature to be curious and to ask questions—and that's what I attempt to do with my video channel. I perpetually seek to inspire curiosity and the pursuit of knowledge.

Why Did I Write This Book?

My goal here is to cover subjects I would like to create videos about, but are too long to contain within the *RealLifeLore* parameters. In a sense, the logic behind why I selected these subjects is no different than what goes on the YouTube channel—only these written pieces are longer and more in-depth.

I decide on topics mainly by brainstorming and thinking about things in a different way. I believe there's a unique angle to every situation and story, and you just have to look at things from a certain perspective to make it come alive. Digging a hole, for example, may be pretty boring to some people—but, if I were to suggest what it might mean to *dig the deepest hole in the world,* then it suddenly becomes pretty fascinating.

I try to explore what can push the boundaries of reality without getting into pure fiction. The boundary of reality is the most interesting place to be when it comes to discussing pretty much anything—whether it's knowing which President had a pet alligator or that Attila the Hun ransomed Rome for 3,000 pounds of pepper (yes, *pepper*) in 408 AD.

In this book, be prepared to explore some of the strangest borders on our planet:

- *What would happen if Charlemagne's Empire or the Persian Empire existed today?*

- *How geographically distant can you be at any time from a Walmart or McDonald's location?*

- *How many countries exist in our world?*

- *Who carries the US nuclear codes?*

As if that's not enough, you'll also receive a tutorial on how to create and establish your very own country! Not a bad promise for a first book, don't you think?

My advice to anyone starting out on a new venture: If you enjoy it, keep doing it. If you are creating something unique that you love, keep working at it and improving it. Integrate the criticism you agree with and discard all the rest. If you listen to your inner voice, dismiss the doubters, and persevere, I believe you will ultimately be successful.

CHAPTER ONE

WHY DO STRANGE BORDERS EXIST?

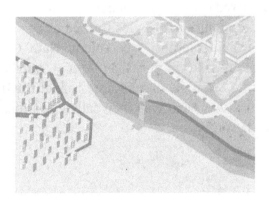

Human society has dense borders—economic, religious, and cultural—inculcated from an early age. We hate change.

—Alejandro Jodorowsky, Chilean director and performer

What is a border, really? In simple terms, a border is where one country ends and another country begins.

Many borders have quite obvious features. They may be rivers, mountain ranges, oceans, or any other substantial geographic barriers. But then there are very strange borders that at face value don't appear to make a lot of sense. Let's begin by talking about countries that are entirely—or almost entirely—surrounded by one single other country.

Lesotho: The Mountain Kingdom

The country of Lesotho is a strange oddity in our world. It's a little smaller than the US state of Maryland, is home to over two million people, and is a completely independent country with its own government and King.

Despite its legal independence, the whole country is completely surrounded by South Africa. This strange situation occurred over a century ago in 1910, when what is today modern South Africa was formed by the British out of four of their colonies: Cape Colony, Natal Colony, Transvaal Colony, and Orange River Colony. Notably absent from this list of colonies, that became part of the Union of South Africa, was what was then called Basutoland—modern day Lesotho.

Map of Lesotho

Why Is Lesotho Known as the "Mountain Kingdom?"

If you were to travel through Lesotho, chances are you'd mainly see mountains. Nearly two-thirds of the entire country consist of mountain ranges of every size and proportion you can imagine.

Lesotho also happens to feature the Highest Altitude Pub in Africa, which is aptly named, as it is nearly 2,900 meters above sea level. Located at the beginning of Sani Pass, it is an ideal place for a cold brew with a view.

The British attempted to include Basutoland within South Africa, but they failed due to the reluctance of the people within the colony. Basutoland would remain a British controlled colony even after South Africa achieved full self- governance in 1931, awkwardly placing a piece of British administered territory right in the middle of a self-governing former colony.

Basutoland finally gained independence from Britain in 1966, but its geographic situation means that the country has been severely influenced by South Africa ever since. All trade that comes into Lesotho has to first go through South Africa. Lesotho is completely landlocked and literally surrounded by South African territory on all sides, so all transportation to or from Lesotho must first go through South Africa. Even air travel has to venture through South African airspace first before it can enter Lesotho, which means that developments in South Africa will inevitably lead to the same occurrences in Lesotho.

But Lesotho isn't the only landlocked country in the world that is entirely surrounded by another country. The next two happen to both be located in Italy.

Italian Frontiers

The first Italian border for discussion is Vatican City, which is a terribly complicated subject all on its own. Vatican City is the smallest internationally recognized, fully sovereign nation on Earth—smaller than Central Park in New York City at 110 acres and having a population around 1,000 citizens. Despite this, however, it's a fully legal, independent country inside the Italian city of Rome with its own borders, as well as its own police force, firefighters, and passports.

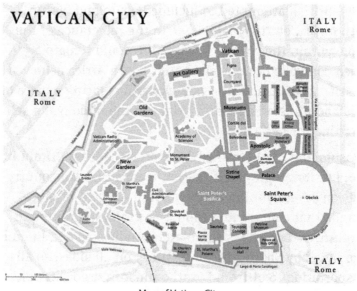

Map of Vatican City

For centuries, the Papacy controlled their own country, known as the Papal States, which controlled a large territory in central Italy. The entire Italian peninsula was divided into dozens of small city-states and regional powers, but that reality began to change in the nineteenth century. Slowly but surely, a united Italian kingdom began to emerge and eventually it reached the point where all of Italy was united into the same kingdom, except for the stubborn Papal States and San Marino. The Kingdom of Italy ended up invading the Papal States in 1860, and then occupied and annexed the rest of the country in 1870, which essentially left the Pope a stateless entity. The Pope controlled no physical territory and, as a result, the relations between the Pope and the Italian government were openly hostile for the next sixty years.

This situation, dubbed "The Roman Question," was finally settled in the 1920's under Benito Mussolini's Fascist government. The Pope was to be granted an area within the city of Rome that would once again serve as his own sovereign territory. The area became what is still today Vatican City and is the last remaining absolute monarchy within Europe. It is legally recognized within the borders of Rome and completely surrounded by modern day Italy.

Bet You Didn't Know These Facts About Vatican City

Vatican City pretty much runs self-sufficiently. It has its own stamps, coinage (imprinted with a portrait of the current Pope), and issues its own passports. It even has its own national soccer team (there known as football), which experienced its first (and rather decisive) win against a representative of Austrian Journalists in 1985.

The Most Serene Republic of San Marino, Italy

The other country completely surrounded by another country is also in Italy: San Marino. As legend has it, the country was founded in 301 AD by a Christian stonemason named Marinus. Its first constitution was written in 1600, making it one of the oldest in world history.

San Marino

San Marino Sports Facts

San Marino is known for an unusual number of professional sports, despite the country's size. It goes without saying soccer (a.k.a. football) is the most popular, but motor sports, basketball, and volleyball are also in the mix. However, its baseball team is the one that has achieved some notoriety, winning the European Cup championships twice—in 2006 and 2008.

San Marino has a population of nearly 33,000 and is the world's fifth smallest country at 23.5 miles long. The capital? San Marino, of course, though the country's largest city is Dogbane. The country has its own stamp and coin systems—both of which are prized by international collectors.

The country must be doing something right in maintaining its independence from Italy, its adjacent border. It has a thriving tourism industry, receiving three million visitors a year. Best of all, the nation's average life expectancy is eighty-three years of age—the third best in the world behind Macau and Monaco.

Some Other Odd Border Facts

1. **North and South Korea:** It would be a grave understatement to say that these two nations do not get along. They have a long history of conflict, which we needn't get into here. While some of their borders are pretty heavily guarded, there is one location in Panmunjom where the countries *aren't even separated by a street*; they are in such close proximity that only a wooden plank is between them and their guarded blue building structures.

Korean DMZ, Panmunjom

2. **Ethiopia and Somalia:** These two countries have a border that is separated by only a flimsy piece of string.

3. **Canada and the United States:** Most people think the Canadian and US border—the longest in the world, stretching over 5,500 miles—is pretty straightforward and peaceful, right? Think again. There are two points that remain in an unresolved state: Machias Seal Island and North Rock between Maine and New Brunswick.

4. **The Mediterranean Sea bordering between Africa and Europe:** This is perhaps the world's most dangerous border, as numerous refugee and migrant boats capsize in the treacherous waters each year. In 2016 alone, around 5,000 deaths occurred in the Mediterranean Sea.

5. **New York Anomalies:** We have room for one tidbit pertaining to American states. Liberty Island and Ellis Island, which symbolize American freedom and liberty, are in New York—right? Not exactly: They are actually located in New Jersey waters. Some of the areas that have been claimed by New York since 1834 were overturned by the US Supreme Court in 1998 and given to New Jersey because these locations had been created by landfill. New Jersey owned the waters and submerged lands around Ellis Island, so the Supreme Court ruled that anything created on those spots to expand the property—even as landfill—was part of their state.

HOW MUCH DO YOU KNOW ABOUT BORDERS?

1. What countries border Israel?

2. What state did the US buy from Mexico for fifteen million dollars?

3. What European nation with thousands of years of history only became officially known as a unified country in 1851?

4. Why did China build its famous Great Wall?

5. Was Korea ever unified?

CHAPTER TWO

WHAT IF HISTORICAL EMPIRES WERE TO REUNITE TODAY?

Merrily sang the monks of Ely
As King Canute came rowing by.
"Row to the shore, knights," said the king,
"And let us hear these churchmen sing."
—English nursery rhyme

Countries and empires come and go throughout human history. Some last for only a brief period of time, such as Alexander the Great's Macedonian Empire—which was essentially dissolved shortly after his death. Others, like the Roman Empire, existed for well over 1,000 years.

Although many of these historic ancient empires no longer exist, their geographical space still does. From a geographical perspective, the world map doesn't change very much over the course of a few hundred years. On the other hand, human civilization changes often—sometimes quite dramatically in just a single year. Borders shift, people migrate, new cities are built, old cities are abandoned, new languages evolve from older languages, and so on. We're in a hyper-globalized world where modern transportation makes it quick and easy to get from here to there and the Internet keeps us connected 24/7 wherever we happen to be (as long as there is a Wi-Fi signal).

Human civilization is incredibly kinetic and prone to changes, so it's interesting to see what historical empires would look like today if they were recreated on their exact historic borders.

What would the Roman Empire look like today in comparison with how it looked in the time of Julius Caesar? How would the populations of past and present compare? How different would the ethnic and linguistic makeups be? Who would be the Emperor or President today in those locations?

The very notion of a "country" is a fairly recent phenomenon. For almost all of human history, the idea of a modern nation state—or even a state at all—simply didn't exist. People generally identified themselves more with their religion, tribe, or family than any notion of a nation.

People have migrated in different ways throughout history, which can significantly change how a particular area on our globe appears to us. For example, what we now consider to be Anatolia and Turkey used to be a largely Greek speaking and Christian practicing region of our planet. Beginning in the eleventh century, however, Anatolia began to be invaded by vast migrations of Turkish peoples.

Over the centuries, the Greek and Christian populations were gradually replaced by the new Turkish speaking and Muslim populations. Today, the land that was the Byzantine Empire circa 555 AD is now overwhelmingly populated by Turks, Arabs, and Muslims. If one were to go back in time to 555 AD, Islam hadn't even come into existence yet.

It's equally as fascinating to see how some regions of the world have changed over time as it is to find those few that have changed very little. In this chapter, we are going to examine three of these historical empires recreated today—the Roman, Vikings, and German empires—assuming no population changes or damage takes place beforehand. We will examine the modern day regions that would make up these empires and explain how the modern forms of these empires would function.

We can leave it up to you to decide whether or not these empires could actually survive as long (or as briefly) as their historical counterparts.

Empire 1: The Roman Empire

What can be said about the Roman Empire that hasn't been said already? Quite a great deal, actually, especially in terms of what a "Roman Empire" might look like today.

The important question is where to begin the investigation. The Roman Empire lasted so long—estimates range between *1,229 to 2,206 years*—and encompassed so much territory—some *2,400 miles east to west*—that any analysis is daunting.

With this in mind, I think it's best to start by listing the countries in existence today that the Roman Empire would encompass: Portugal, Spain, France, Belgium, Luxembourg, Italy, Switzerland, Austria, Slovenia, Croatia, Bosnia-

Herzegovina, Montenegro, Albania, Macedonia, Kosovo, Greece, Bulgaria, Turkey, Lebanon, Israel, and Palestine.

There are also other countries the empire would *almost* entirely cover: England (including Wales), Iraq, Jordan, and Egypt (with one province divided in three in one area).

And there's more—countries with *partial* territory in the Empire: the Netherlands, Germany, Slovakia, Hungary, Romania (over 90 percent), Ukraine, Russia, Georgia, Armenia (over 90 percent) Azerbaijan (over 90 percent), Iran, Kuwait, Saudi Arabia, Libya, Tunisia (over 90 percent), Algeria, and Morocco.

You may be asking: What areas *didn't* the Romans conquer and possess to at least some degree? Here are just a few: China (though they did have a settlement here and there), Ireland, Scotland, and Japan.

Did the Romans Reach the Americas?

Shockingly, some historians believe the answer is yes! A discovery made on Oak Island off the coast of Novia Scotia, Canada may reveal that the Romans landed in North America a full millennium before Columbus's arrival. A sword, inexplicable ancient burial mounds, coins, and crossbow bolts found on the Island have been tested and proven to date back to ancient Rome and match materials and metals used by the Romans from that time. A nearby underwater shipwreck is being examined to determine its origins, though some historians have already drawn conclusions that it is Roman in origin. Who knows what other Roman presence has yet to be found around the globe....

This is an image of the Roman Empire at the height of her power in the year 117 AD when it owned approximately 10 percent of the world's territory. Despite such might, Rome was unable to sustain its forces over such wide areas of land, and the spread of Christianity was beginning to unravel the Roman way of life. She gradually lost power over time, suffering defeats in waves across Roman lands from invading Germanic Goths. Eventually, the Roman Empire faded, leaving a mountainous archaeological legacy throughout the Mediterranean and Europe.

The Roman Empire 117 AD.

What would a country with the same borders as the old Roman Empire look like in the twenty-first century? What if all of the territory of the Roman Empire suddenly united tomorrow and recreated the country in a modern form? It goes without saying that this is outrageously impossible, as there is no way that you could possibly convince Spain,

England, Turkey, Syria, and other countries to unite as the same country. Crimea would get a little more awkward than it already is, but let's suspend our disbelief for a moment.

So first off, this is a modern map and these are what the borders of the Roman Empire would look like were they to come back into existence. In total, fifty-three different countries would lose all or some of their territory to the Empire, which would span over six million square kilometers in size. This sounds really impressive, but the Empire would only be the seventh largest country in the world. It would be slightly larger than India, but smaller than Australia and Brazil. Russia, meanwhile, would be nearly three times the size of the Roman Empire. But size isn't necessarily everything.

If we examine the population of this hypothetical empire, it would be roughly 711 million or about 10 percent of the total global population. The original ancient Roman Empire had ten times fewer citizens at about seventy million people, but it is important to put this into perspective and note that back then this was 21 percent of the entire world's population! The modern Empire's population would be enough to place it third in terms of population size, but both India and China would retain higher populations. The empire would, however, have more than double the population of the United States and boast some impressive cities.

If we were to speculate on a hypothetical capital for the Empire, we might settle on Istanbul, which was a historic capital back when it was known as Constantinople. Today, the population of Istanbul is around 14,600,000, making it by far the largest city in this empire. At the height of the city during the actual Empire in 500 AD, the population was 450,000. Even earlier, in 100 AD, the city of Rome was the first city in world history to reach a population of one million people. Although Rome today has a population of well over two million, there would still be much bigger cities within the borders of the Empire today, such as Cairo, London, Baghdad, and Alexandria.

At first blush, it might seem like such a huge country would have the number one economy in the world today. While it would be a powerhouse, it wouldn't quite reach that level. All of the Roman territory combined would yield a GDP of $15.99 trillion USD, some $2 trillion less than the US, which has less than half of the population.

Was Julius Caesar the First Roman Emperor?

Technically, he was not. Gaius Julius Caesar was considered many things and had several titles throughout his life, but he was murdered without ever having been dubbed "emperor." He was referred to as either a god, the consul, or "dictator for life."

Caesar had three wives and several lovers (including Cleopatra VII, the Egyptian ruler), but contrary to myth, none of his blood offspring ever succeeded him as the leader of Rome. Caesarion ("little Caesar"), his son with Cleopatra, shared the rule of Egypt with his mother and then reigned by himself after her death. Caesar's daughter, Julia, is believed to have died while delivering her child, who also perished.

The first official emperor of Rome was Augustus Caesar: adopted son and grand-nephew of Julius Caesar. During his reign, Emperor Augustus doubled the size of the Empire, bringing in Egypt, northern Spain, the Alps, and a chunk of the Balkans.

The differences in per capita income would be even more shocking. The modern Roman Empire would have territory in wealthier areas such as England, France,

and Germany—but also in more impoverished areas
such as Iraq, Armenia, and Libya. For this reason, the
average income of citizens within the Empire would be
around $24,623 dollars, which is toward the lower end
of the spectrum at fifty-second in the world—ahead of
Kazakhstan, but behind Latvia.

With a large GDP and population, however, the Empire
would have a significant standing army. Averaging all of the
active military personnel in the territories within the Empire
and adding them together, it would total about 2,771,000—
making it the largest standing force in the world.

The final two big questions we have left to examine
with this country are: (1) What would be the dominant
languages? and (2) What would be the dominant religions?

The most widely spoken language within the country
would be Arabic at 32 percent of the population. French
would be the second most spoken language with about 14
percent of the population. Turkish would be third at about
9.5 percent, followed by Italian and English.

As for religion, Muslims would be the largest religious
group inside the modern Empire, making up 44.6 percent
of the total population (42.2 percent Sunni Muslims and
2.4 percent Shia Muslims). Interestingly, this would make
the modern Roman Empire the largest Muslim nation in
the world.

Christians would be the second largest group, collectively
forming 39.3 percent of the population. Of that, Catholics
would comprise 25.2 percent of the total population, while
Orthodox Christians would be 8.2 percent and Protestants
5.6 percent. These numbers would make the modern Roman
Empire the world's largest Christian nation as well. Jews
would only form about 1 percent of the total population,

while Atheists, Agnostics, and the non-religious would make up 10.5 percent of the country.

Phew—that takes care of the Roman Empire. Now it's time to turn our focus to another gigantic ancient empire, which happens to have the same name as a certain NFL football team in Minnesota.

Empire 2: The Viking Realm

The Vikings were Nordic seafarers who explored, raided, and traded across a vast area stretching from Russia to North America between the eighth and eleventh centuries. They originally hailed from modern day Scandinavia, but in a few short centuries had expanded and settled lands as far away as Britain, Ireland, Normandy, Russia, and even modern day Canada. In actuality, they were the first known Europeans to "discover" the New World.

Contrary to popular belief, never at any time during all of these centuries was there such a thing as a "Viking Empire." The people we today call Vikings were never united into a single force, nation state, or empire. They were a mixture of various chiefs and kings, each with their own agendas and ambitions.

That being said, we are going to look at two separate versions of a modern day Viking realm being united. The first one, in the early eleventh century, is the closest the Vikings were to resembling a unified empire: The North Sea Empire. And then, just for fun, we'll add in all the regions that were actually settled by the Norse people during the Viking Age.

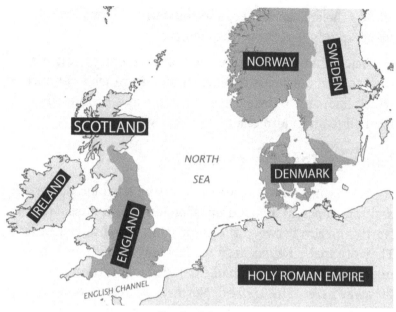

King Cnut's Empire

This North Sea Empire was ruled by the Danish King, Cnut the Great, between 1016 and 1035. As you can see from the map, this empire spanned much of modern day Norway, Sweden, Denmark, England, and Scotland. These were the regions that were ruled directly by Cnut as King. However, he also ruled territories highlighted in dark gray as vassal or client territories. Taking both of these into account, Cnut ruled an empire that essentially spanned from modern day Dublin to Stockholm, which would have made him certainly one of the most powerful men in the world at his time—yet hardly anyone outside Scandinavia has ever heard of him.

King Chute's Tomb

The remains of King Chute—who was also known as
King Knute or *King Canute*—are believed to be inside a
chest housed in Winchester Cathedral in England. If
true, his bones may be mixed with those of a number of
other kings, as well as Cnut's wife, Emma. The chest has
recently been removed from its position in a stone wall
in the cathedral and taken for laboratory screening of its
contents and for restoration of the chest itself.

If Cnut's empire were to magically come into existence
today, it would certainly be one of the world's most powerful
countries. But let's examine exactly what it would look like
and how it would probably fit into our current world.

To begin with, if we include the vassal territories in the
empire, seven different countries would lose some or all
of their territory. Mainland Denmark would be the only
country that would be 100 percent absorbed into the empire,
which would be fitting since Cnut was born a Dane. The
entire island of Great Britain would be absorbed as well,
which is almost the entire United Kingdom—save for of
Northern Ireland and the British Overseas Territories.
Norway, Sweden, and Ireland would lose significant areas
to the empire as well, including all three of those countries'
capital cities of Oslo, Stockholm, and Dublin. Finally,
Germany and Poland would lose relatively minor territories
to the empire.

The Empire would share borders with what remains of
Norway and Sweden in Scandinavia, maintain two small
in mainland Europe with both Germany and Poland and,
finally, have various short borders with the Republic of
Ireland, due to the many exclaves of Viking territory there.

The Vikings' Day Job

When they weren't out at sea, the Vikings were farmers at home. They lived off what the farms could produce and raise—both vegetables and animals—and often consumed stewed fish or meat. Their libation of choice was mead, a concoction made with fermented honey.

Contrary to popular lore, the Vikings were not slovenly, ill-mannered people. Archaeologists have found plenty of tools to suggest that they used standard eating utensils, groomed themselves, and even dyed their hair blonde, since this color was highly admired at the time.

The population of this Northern European Empire would make it the largest country in Europe in terms of people—some 82,405,000 citizens, which would place it just ahead of Germany with a population of 81,459,000. If we were to take the entire rest of the world into consideration, then the North Sea Empire would be the 16th most populated nation. It would be just ahead of The Democratic Republic of the Congo and Germany, but it would remain just behind the populations of Egypt and Vietnam. Comparing the populations to very large countries, the North Sea Empire would have about 25 percent of the population of the United States and only 6 percent of the population of China.

In terms of sheer geographic size, the North Sea Empire would also be the second largest country in Europe behind Russia in terms of size and population. The Empire would be a moderately sized country compared to the rest of the world, achieving forty-fifth place globally—just ahead of Ukraine, but remaining a smidge behind South Sudan. So the Empire would be very large compared to its European neighbors, but not relative to the rest of the world.

You may be asking: What would the restored North Sea Empire's economy look like? Adding up the GDP figures of all the countries, regions, counties, and cities within this Empire provides our answer. The North Sea Empire would have a Nominal GDP of $3.634 trillion USD, which would place it as the fourth largest economy in the world. This is particularly interesting because, while Germany is much smaller in size, it would have a very similar population and a comparable economy. The German economy as of this writing has a nominal value, according to the International Monetary Fund, of $3.4949 trillion USD dollars, which is only a small percentage below what we estimated for the North Sea Empire. While the North Sea Empire would surpass the German economy to achieve fourth place, it would not even come close to Japan in third place at $4.73 trillion USD.[1]

This further would mean that the nominal GDP per capita for the North Sea Empire would be pretty high at a value of $44,293. GDP per capita is often used as a way to tell what the living standards inside a country would look like. This system has its flaws because, while it only shows us averages, the living standards inside this country would be pretty high compared to global averages. The North Sea Empire would be placed with the thirteenth highest GDP per capita in the world ahead of the United Kingdom, which means that on average UK citizens would slightly benefit from this arrangement economically with everything else remaining equal.

San Marino would be slightly above the North Sea Empire in GDP per capita, and slightly above that would be Sweden.

---

1 For reference, the Chinese economy is the second largest in the world at $11.392 trillion USD, while the American economy is the largest in this scenario at $18.562 trillion USD.

In fact, Sweden, Denmark, and Norway all have higher GDP per capita than the North Sea Empire would have already, which means that the citizens within these parts of the Empire would actually stand to lose economically on average. Meanwhile, the citizens in the UK parts of the Empire would stand to benefit economically on average.

England would certainly be the true powerhouse and center of this Empire. More than two thirds of the entire Empire's population would come from England alone, whereas 64 percent of the Empire's economy would come from England. Out of the top twenty largest cities in the Empire, twelve or 60 percent of them would all be located in England including the two biggest, London and Birmingham.

Scandinavia, meanwhile, would only have four or 20 percent of the top twenty largest cities, but among them would be Stockholm—the third largest city in the Empire. The only city located outside of either Scandinavia or the British Isles among the top twenty would be Szczecin, Poland, which is far down at sixteenth place.

If we had to speculate on a suitable capital for the Empire, we couldn't really tell from history. The Empire had no common capital city 1,000 years ago, so by default it probably would be London—the largest city and the one with the best infrastructure.

Clearly, the diplomacy of this Empire suddenly coming back into existence would be complicated. It would be one of the most powerful countries in the world with the largest economy in Europe, and the fourth largest in the world. The Empire would likely dominate European affairs.

Viking Ships

Many people have the romantic image of Viking ships being imposing, gigantic, and heavily decorated with dragonheads at the tip. The truth of the matter is that the Vikings had a range of different ships for various purposes and only a few led by their most important leaders (e.g., kings) featured a dragonhead. The two main types of ships were long ships (used for trade as well as warfare) and knars (used for carrying cargo and/or lengthy voyages, such as across an ocean).

In July 2017, a Viking knarr was discovered near the Mississippi River, which demonstrates that the Vikings entered even deeper into the Americas than previously believed. Experts believe the ship would have held about twenty to thirty passengers and dates the wreck between 990 and 1050 AD.

I would speculate that it wouldn't become a member state of the European Union, owing to the fact that the entire United Kingdom is soon going to leave it anyway—and Norway has never been a part of it, either. The only EU territories within the Empire would be Denmark and chunks of Ireland, Germany, Sweden, and Poland, but those would all likely leave the EU because the rest of the empire would be out of it.

If the Empire were to continue a Viking inspired foreign policy, perhaps it would begin by raiding the European Union coastlines. This could conceivably start a kind of European Cold War between the EU and the Empire. The Empire would also probably begin raids into Russia as the historical Vikings did, which would raise tensions there.

The Empire would benefit from enormous gas reserves, thanks to the offshore oil rigs possessed by Norway. This would make them somewhat independent from the oil shocks that could occur from Russia or the Middle East. The Empire would also be in possession of all of the United Kingdom's nuclear weapons, making it a major world threat.

The Empire would have some weaknesses as well. The economic imbalance between the Scandinavians and the majority population in Britain would be worrisome, as well as the fact that the Empire would probably be largely centered around London and Britain—much to the chagrin of the Irish, Scandinavian, German, and Polish populations. Poland and Germany would likely not tolerate part of their territory being taken from them and could easily resist, as these are small chunks of land. Sweden, Norway, and Ireland likely could not resist the empire, since a large portion of their territories would be taken into the Empire, including all three of their capital cities. However, it would be entirely plausible that underground rebellions would take place in all them.

If the Empire could overcome these differences, it would certainly become a potential superpower and likely be the dominant force in Europe. Her only rivals for global supremacy would be the United States, Russia, or China. We could spend an entire book talking about just the future diplomacy of some of these nations, but it's now time to move on and analyze our next empire.

Empire 3: The German Empire

The German Empire existed in Europe between the Prussian victory and unification of Germany in 1871 until the nation's defeat in the First World War decades later in 1918. During its brief period of existence, the Empire was the dominant power in Europe and was well on its way to becoming a potential superpower. Had Germany achieved victory in World War I, the twentieth century might have become a German-dominated century instead of American.

The German Empire possessed the most powerful army in the world at the time, the second most powerful Navy, the highest number of Nobel Prizes awarded in science, and a rapidly growing industrial base.

Wilhelm II: The Last Kaiser

Kaiser Wilhelm II was the ruler of Germany and King of Prussia for three decades between 1888 through 1918. Although his father (Frederick III) was Kaiser for a brief period, his mother (Victoria) was actually British—the eldest daughter of Queen Victoria.

Kaiser Wilhelm II was a controversial figure throughout his lifetime and his memory has receded into history. On the one hand, he increased Germany's power, economy, education, arts, and scientific status a great deal up through World War I; after that, however, he fell into disfavor and was forced to abdicate in exile. It was not well known (until this writing, of course) that one of his arms was paralyzed from nerve damaged at birth—a fact he tried to conceal.

In short, it was a true juggernaut of a country—but what would it look like if all of a sudden it were to be recreated down to its exact borders just prior to the disaster of the First World War?

The German Empire in 1914 possessed territories stretching far outside of the borders of present day Germany. The Empire held lands in modern day France, Belgium, Denmark, the Czech Republic, Poland, Lithuania, and Russia—not to mention extensive colonies in Africa and

Asia. We are not going to discuss these colonies, however, since we are focusing on what the German Empire would look like in a modern day Europe.

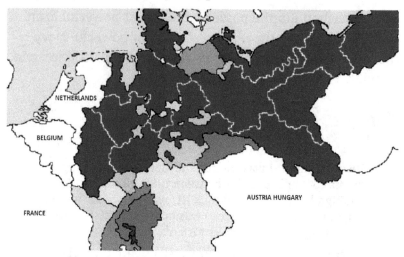

German Empire in 1914

Modern Germany

Present day Germany makes up only about two thirds of the same territory in Europe that the German Empire occupied. The Empire would have a large population of 102,809,000, which would make it by far the most populous nation in Europe, excluding Russia.

These are the countries and regions that would make up the recreated 1914 German Empire in Europe:

- Germany (all)

- France (Alsace, most of Lorraine)

- Denmark (South Jutland)

- Poland (provinces of West Pomerania, Lubusz, Lower Silesia, Pomerania, most of Warmian-Masurian, Greater Poland, Opole and Kuyavian Pomerania)

- Russia (Kaliningrad Oblast)

- Lithuania (Counties of Šilutė, Klaipėda, Neringa Municipality, Klaipeda City and Palanga City)

- Belgium (small territory in the east)

- Czechia (Czech Silesia)

The ethnic diversity of the recreated German Empire would be: 72 percent Germans; 16 percent Poles; 2.8 percent French; and 9.2 percent everyone else. The religious breakdown changes significantly in the recreated German Empire: 44 percent Catholic (large increase because of Polish territories); 27 percent Protestant; 24 percent none; 3 percent Islam; and 2 percent all other.

The Nominal GDP of the recreated German Empire would be $3.745 trillion USD, the fourth highest in the world.

However, the GDP of Germany alone today is $3.371 trillion USD and is already the fourth highest in the world—so this increase doesn't drastically change things very much in terms of global power.

The Nominal GDP per capita of the Empire is $36,427 per person. This is lower than the current GDP per capita of modern Germany, which is $41,267. It is therefore reasonable to assume that Germany would have to pay a large amount of money to develop several of these new territories in Poland and Russia to maximize their economic output.

Assuming all regions and territories keep their current percentage of GDP spent on defending their mother country (e.g., Poland spends 2 percent, which means that amount of the Polish territories have been allocated to the recreated German Empire's defense spending). The military budget therefore amounts to $46.473 billion USD. This gives the recreated German Empire the eighth highest military budget in the world, moving it ahead of Japan but lagging behind both the UK and France. (The United States is at number one by far in any scenario.) This isn't a drastic increase because Germany currently has the ninth highest military budget in the world at $43.8 billion USD.

The recreated German Empire would reobtain several cities. For our purposes, we would restore their old German names as in the following examples:

- Szczecin becomes *Stettin*

- Gdańsk becomes *Danzig*

- Wrocław becomes *Breslau*

- Poznań becomes *Posen*

- Kaliningrad becomes *Königsberg*

- Klaipėda becomes *Memel*

- The province of Alsace-Lorraine renamed to Elsaß (Elsass) becomes *Lothringen*

However, the largest cities in the recreated Empire would be:

1. Berlin

2. Hamburg

3. Munich

4. Cologne

5. Frankfurt

6. Wrocław (Breslau)

7. Stuttgart

8. Düsseldorf

9. Dortmund

10. Essen

11. Leipzig

12. Bremen

13. Dresden

14. Poznań (Posen)

15. Hanover

16. Nuremberg

17. Duisburg

18. Gdańsk (Danzig)

19. Szczecin (Stettin)

20. Bochum

Among the top ten largest cities, only one of them would be from any of these new territories. The capital and largest city of the Empire would be Berlin, just as it was during the original German Empire.

A recreated German Empire would violate several international treaties. The Treaty on the Final Settlement With Respect to Germany was signed in 1990 between West Germany and East Germany, the United States, Soviet Union, France, and the United Kingdom. In the treaty, the USSR, the US, the UK, and France renounced all occupation rights they held in Germany, allowing West and East Germany to reunite with each other to form the modern Federal Republic of Germany. In exchange, Germany renounced her right to ever having nuclear, biological, or chemical weapons.

Most importantly, Germany agreed to permanently recognize her international borders as they were then and are now. This specifically meant the new border with Poland was deemed permanent, and Germany renounced all claims to any former German territory. Germany is constitutionally prohibited from accepting any application for incorporation into Germany from any territory outside her present borders, which means that the recreation of the German Empire to its 1914 borders is legally impossible.

Without a doubt, Germany expanding to these territories would lead to a war that would be pretty pointless. The acquisition of these territories would do very little to expand Germany's power. Her economy would remain in the current fourth place globally, and the new territories are filled with people who are not Germans.

Even so, it's a fascinating exercise to demonstrate that acquisition of these old territories would be a nonsensical, fruitless endeavor and would do very little to help Germany in relation to the massive consequences and costs of doing so.

HOW MUCH DO YOU KNOW ABOUT EMPIRES?

1. What was the world's largest empire?

2. Genghis Khan ruled over what massive empire in the thirteenth Century?

3. What is believed to be the longest running empire dynasty in history?

4. Was French emperor Napoleon Bonaparte short in real life?

5. What concubine became the most powerful empress in world history?

CHAPTER THREE

HOW FAR AWAY CAN YOU GET FROM CERTAIN THINGS?

Everywhere is within walking distance if you have the time.

—Stephen Wright, comedian

There are some things in this world that you may be afraid of: the ocean, bears, sharks, diseases, other people, heights, spiders, or any number of other things. Some people even fear domestic cats, which is known as *ailurophobia*. (One such famous ailurophobe happened to be Napoleon Bonaparte.)

Naturally, if you are afraid of something you want to remain as far away from it as possible. You may be asking: Geographically speaking, what is the farthest distance I can be from anyone living or inanimate thing?

The Farthest Points in the World

If you have seen any of my YouTube videos, you are likely familiar with one I did that covered how far away you can possibly get from every other person on the planet. In other words, where are the loneliest places on the planet? I won't go into too much detail about that here, but the answer that I gave in the video is a place in the middle of the Pacific Ocean called Point Nemo.

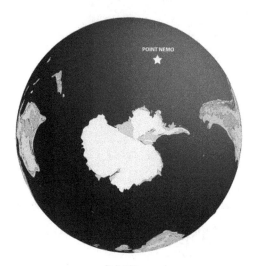

Point Nemo

If for whatever reason you found yourself way out at Point Nemo, the nearest possible land (and person) to you would be located 2,688 kilometers at the Easter Islands. The fastest time anybody has ever made it to Point Nemo on a boat while starting at land was over seven days. Of course, if you were on a raft heading to Point Nemo and didn't know what you were doing—well, it would take you *a lot longer* than those seven days. You would be so geographically isolated that every so often when the International Space Station would orbit above you, the astronauts onboard would actually be the closest humans to you at a distance of 400 kilometers.

Let's say the ocean is your biggest fear, not isolation. Maybe you're terrified of sharks, giant squid, tsunamis, or whatever else may lurk in the dark depths of the ocean. Whatever the reason behind your fear of the ocean, you just know you want to stay far away from it. But what is the farthest location away from it?

The Farthest Point from an Ocean: North America and South America

Naturally, the farthest place from the ocean would have to be the center of a land mass, a large continent. What we are then left wondering is: the center of *which* land mass? Is it North America? Africa? Europe? This is difficult to discern just by looking at a map, but no need to worry—that's why you're reading this book!

Let's start with North America: What is the farthest you could be from an ocean in this continent? This isn't as easy as it seems: In fact, according to NOAA (the National Oceanic and Atmospheric Administration), about 39 percent of the US population lives in a county that has a direct coastline.

How to Determine the Farthest Place from You

Have you ever been so upset with someone you wish to get as far away from him or her as possible? If distance is what you seek, that information is now right at your fingertips—you don't have to look at a map, do any math, or even use a GPS! The web site furthestcity.com tabulates this for you, located at: http://furthestcity.com/. The one caveat is that the site only includes cities with a population of 100,000 or more.

If you happen to be in New Haven, CT, for example, a couple of clicks will tell you that the farthest city is some 18,711 kilometers away: Perth, Australia. If you are on the West Coast of the US in LA, the farthest is a French island some 18,429 kilometers away, Saint Paul, Réunion, located in the Indian Ocean.

The point in the US you would be looking for is inside the state of South Dakota, just eleven kilometers north of the town of Allen. It's in the middle of nowhere and few people outside the area have ever heard of it, but it's the farthest geographic point on the North American continent from any ocean at about 1,650 kilometers away. If you're curious to search the coordinates and find out how to get there, type these digits on your smartphone: 43° 21′ 36″ N, 101° 58′ 12″ W.

Eleven kilometers north of Allen, SD

Next let's shuffle way down south and visit the most landlocked place in South America. If you happen to ever visit these coordinates 14° 3′ 0″ S, 56° 51′ 0″ W, you'll find yourself in the middle of a remote farm in the west of Brazil, and you'll also be the farthest away from any ocean on the continent.

The Farthest from an Ocean: The Pole of Inaccessibility

Now let's combine both the European and Asian continents into one distinct continent to reveal the most difficult place for you to visit on our list.

The coordinates for this spot are: 46° 17′ 0″ N, 86° 40′ 0″ E. It is located inside far western China close to the border with Kazakhstan. This place, known as the "Pole of Inaccessibility," is so landlocked that the closest point to an ocean is a massive 2,645 kilometers (1,644 miles) away. To put this into perspective, imagine the distance between San Francisco, California and Little Rock, Arkansas.

For Europeans, the distance is about the same as from Lisbon, Portugal to Lodz, Poland. Imagine going that entire distance without ever reaching an ocean!

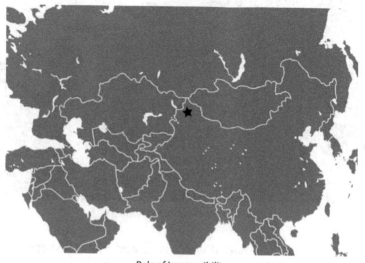

Pole of Inaccessibility

The Pole of Inaccessibility is also difficult to reach because it's quite literally in the middle of nowhere. Its nearest towns are a place called Suluk, ten kilometers to the east; Xazgat, about twenty kilometers to the west; and Hoxtolgay, about fifty kilometers to the northwest. You can drive along a road from any of these villages and get within 600 meters of the spot from the closest road, which isn't all that far. The challenging part, however, is getting into one of those towns and then driving to this position. If you're looking for a place that's free from vehicle noise and traffic, then stick around for when we talk about how far away you can possibly get from a road!

The Farthest from an Ocean: Australia and Africa

The final two continents for our discussion are Australia and Africa. If you're in the former, you'd probably guess that the farthest point from the ocean would be somewhere in the Outback desert—and you'd be correct. This place is so remote that it may actually be even more difficult to reach than the point in Eurasia we just finished discussing. You can check out the coordinates at 23° 10' 12" S, 132° 16' 12" E to note that it's located only by dirt roads that are 920 kilometers (570 miles) away from the nearest coastline. The nearest town is a place called Papunya, about 30 kilometers (19 miles) to the southwest.

Australian Outback

Finally, let's move on to the farthest point away from the ocean in Africa. That location would be at the coordinates 5° 39' 0" N, 26° 10' 12" E located in the Central African Republic, 1,814 kilometers (1,127 miles) away from the nearest coast. It's not in a particularly remote place of the continent, as it's near the country's border with Sudan and the Democratic Republic of the Congo.

How Close Can You Be to Space While Standing on Earth's Surface?

Is there a real method of determining this? No cheating: rockets, airplanes, balloons, or anything else above the ground don't count, as you must stay on the surface of our planet to get an accurate answer.

So, let's do a little bit of exploration here. First, we need to define where outer space actually begins.

This isn't an easy matter because there is no firm universally agreed upon boundary to mark the beginning of space and the end of Earth. The closest standard point is a region called the Karman Line, which is at an altitude of 100 kilometers (62 miles) above sea level. This is an internationally accepted definition of where outer space begins, though oddly it doesn't seem that far away. Sixty-two miles is a distance that can easily be driven in just an hour if the same distance was on a vertical highway with no traffic. Parts of Pennsylvania, such as Bensalem Township, are only 64 miles to New York City. Imagine being able to drive an hour straight up and, suddenly, you are in space!

What Is the Nearest Hospitable Planet Next to Earth?

The verdict on this one is unlikely to be out any time soon. Scientists estimate that there might be as many as *40 billion planets*, known as exoplanets, around the size of Earth that orbit stars with properties similar to our sun. The red dwarf star Proxima Centauri is the closest star to Earth (about 4.25 light years), but the exoplanets around it are likely inhospitable. That leaves the Alpha Centauri star system, which is about 4.37 light years from our sun and has three stars—two of which (known as A and B) may have up to an 85 percent chance of sustaining an Earth-like hospital world.

So, what is the closest spot on Earth to the Karman Line? It's logical to think that it would be at the top of the tallest mountain in the world. Mount Everest is quite high at 8,848 meters (29,029 feet) above sea level. In fact, it is so unbelievably high that commercial airline planes generally avoid flying near it. The average altitude of a commercial airline is 11,887 meters (39,000 feet), which is only about 10,000 feet higher than the mountain. When visibility is poor due to snowstorms or other bad weather, Mount Everest could pose a very real and terrifying crash site for an airplane.

Despite that, 8,848 meters is only 8.848 percent of the way up to space. Even still, Mount Everest is high enough to penetrate into the Earth's stratosphere, which exposes the top of it to the jet stream, where winds can approach a staggering 280 kilometers per hour (or 175 miles per hour).

What Is the Farthest Entity from Earth Detected in Space?

If you really want to get far away from it all, maybe the best place to consider is a recently discovered galaxy, MACS0647-JD, which is about 13.3 billion light years away. This galaxy came into existence about 420 million years after the Big Bang and is believed to hold around one billion stars.

That's pretty close to space, but you can actually get a little closer by climbing up another mountain: Mount Chimborazo in Ecuador. It has an elevation of 6,263 meters (20,548 feet). While that may not be as high above sea level as Mount Everest, the difference lies in its location.

Mount Chimborazo, Ecuador

You see, the Earth isn't actually a perfect sphere. The planet bulges out slightly along the equator from the rest of the planet. If you are standing along the equator, you're technically a little further out than the rest of humanity standing outside the equator. This effect becomes especially pronounced at Mount Chimborazo, since it's a high mountain that happens to be situated directly on the equator. As a result, the summit on the mountain is the farthest point on the entire planet from the Earth's center—further away than even Everest.

That being said, Mount Chimborazo doesn't reach into the stratosphere the same way Everest does. In theory, while Chimborazo is further away from the Earth's center of mass, Everest still remains closer to space above. Unless you hop on a plane or in a balloon and decide to stay on your feet on some kind of stable surface that is connected to the ground, Everest is the closest to space that you're ever going to get.

HOW MUCH DO YOU KNOW ABOUT PROXIMITY?

1. What country is nearest to Australia?

2. What place is closest to the equator?

3. What birds fly highest in the world?

4. How long would it take a person to walk a light year?

5. What is the closest distance the Earth ever gets to the sun?

CHAPTER FOUR

HOW MANY COUNTRIES ARE THERE IN THE WORLD—NOBODY KNOWS!

Every country is like a particular person. America is like a belligerent adolescent boy. Canada is like an intelligent, thirty-five-year-old woman Australia is like Jack Nicholson. It comes right up to you and laughs very hard in your face in a highly threatening and engaging manner.

—Douglas Adams, English writer and humorist

If somebody were to ask you how many countries there were in the world, how might you answer? You'd probably find a map and spend about ten minutes counting all the countries that you see, right? (Or, you'd cut to the chase and Google it—but let's suppose you don't have wireless at the time.) The problem with that method is that, depending on which map you're using, you'll get many different answers.

The answer to this question depends entirely on whom you're asking—and your personal definition of a country. The most common definition for a country can be taken from the 1933 Montevideo Convention on the Rights and Duties of States, which states that the area must fit the following criteria:

1. It must have a permanent population.

2. It must possess a defined territory.

3. There must be an established and operating government.

4. It must have the capacity to enter into relations with other states.

The first sentence of article three inside the treaty explicitly states that "the political existence of a state is independent of recognition by the other states." If a country refuses to acknowledge the existence of another country, therefore, it doesn't necessarily mean that it's not a country. With this in mind, how are you supposed to figure out how many countries truly exist?

If you were to walk into the United Nations and count how many countries are present, you would come up with an answer of 195 countries in the world. (And yes, Google offers "195" as the answer as well.) But even that number is a little off for two reasons. First, Vatican City—which is widely considered to be a fully independent country—has never joined the United Nations as an official member.[2]

---

2 Vatican City is a complicated situation best saved for another time. However, it is worth noting that the Holy See—a distinct entity from the Vatican City country and an independent sovereign entity—is, at the very least, considered a "UN observer."

The second problem: Technically, there are only 193 countries that are UN member states. The other two entities would be the Holy See (see footnote) and the State of Palestine, which are considered non-member observer states. This leads us into the bizarre realm of entities that are countries according to the definition provided at the beginning of this chapter, but have limited recognition as being such. During the following discussions on countries, please keep in mind this definition: It will prove to be most important in our investigation.

Palestine, Israel, and Kosovo

It's time for us to get a bit controversial. Whenever the Middle East comes into play, it's always best practice to avoid taking any political (and certainly not religious) sides. Let's just stick with the facts and the definition of a country.

The states with the greatest controversy about whether they are "countries" are: Palestine, Israel, and Kosovo. 136 (or about 70 percent of UN member states) officially recognize Palestine as an official country, while the remaining 30 percent of member states do not. That said, Palestine is not an official member of the UN. Countries such as Israel, the United States, Canada, Australia, the UK, France, and Germany do not recognize Palestine as an official country, so you won't be seeing it on many maps generated by these UN members.

On the other side of the equation, Israel is considered a full UN member state. In spite of this fact, thirty-one UN member states—notably, Iran, Saudi Arabia, Pakistan, Indonesia, North Korea, and Cuba—do not recognize Israel as a legitimate country.

Can a Country Disappear?

While it's doubtful an entire country can "vanish" in this day and age, there are quite a few that changed names and/or territories in the twentieth century. In order of dissolution, these are the ten: Yugoslavia (1992; now broken up into Slovenia, Croatia, Bosnia, Serbia, Macedonia, and Montenegro); Czechoslovakia (1992; now divided as the Czech Republic and Slovakia); the Union of Soviet Socialist Republic (1991, now known as the Republics of Russia); East Germany (1990, now integrated into Germany); South Vietnam (1975, now assimilated into Vietnam); Sikkim[3] (1975, now part of India); United Arab Republic (1971, now back to what it had been—Egypt and Syria); Tibet (1951, now part of China); Ottoman Empire (1922, now mostly Turkey although some lands went elsewhere); Austro-Hungary (1918, which, subsequent to WWI, was broken up into Austria, Hungary, Czechoslovakia, and Yugoslavia with some segments handed to Poland, Romania, and Italy).

And then we come to the strange case of Kosovo, which is located in the Balkans in Europe. Interestingly, if you were to compare the maps of countries that officially recognize Palestine to the countries that officially recognize Kosovo, they would be almost entirely opposite. 110 UN member states recognize Kosovo as an independent country, while the remaining eighty-three believe it is part of Serbia.

---

3 Sikkim is major anomaly. Located in the Himalayans between India and China, this country was not much bigger than the state of Rhode Island. It stood as a monarchy (or various teeny-tiny monarchies) for centuries until it finally became part of India in 1975.

Kosovo

Serbia has long insisted that Kosovo is a rebellious province of its nation. Some countries, such as Russia, China, and India have supported the Serbian position, whereas others, such as the United States, the United Kingdom, France, and Germany have supported Kosovo's independence. Like Palestine, it is not considered a full member of the United Nations.

The China Syndrome

China is a whole other matter when it comes to how it figures into the world country count. The problem is that there are separate entities that both refer to themselves as "China." The first is the more familiar People's Republic of China (PRC), which is what most people think of when they say "China." This is the Communist China that is gigantic;

it boasts the world's second biggest economy and the world's largest population.

The other China is the Republic of China (ROC), which is otherwise known as Taiwan since the government exists only on that island. This current situation dates back over a century and is complex, to say the least.

ROC and PRC

Here is a simplified history lesson. The ROC was established back in 1912 after the collapse of the Qing dynasty in China. The ROC then was much larger than modern day China, taking up all of present day Mongolia in addition to other territories in modern Russia, India, and Myanmar. The government became a nationalist dictatorship under the authority of Chiang Kai Shek in 1928. Shortly afterwards, a civil war broke out between the Nationalists and the Communists. The Civil War between the two sides came to a brief halt in 1937 when the Empire of Japan launched a full-scale invasion of China.

The Nationalists and Communists inside China briefly set aside their differences and joined forces against their common Japanese enemy. When the Japanese surrendered unconditionally in 1945, the island of Taiwan was given back to the ROC. Taiwan had been forcefully annexed by the Japanese decades earlier, in 1895. Once the common enemy was defeated, the old enemies soon resumed their fight for control of China and civil war broke out.

The war dragged on bitterly for another four years until 1949 when the Communists emerged victorious and established the PRC in the mainland. The nationalist ROC forces fled the mainland to the island of Taiwan that same year to continue their government.

From that island, the ROC has continued to maintain their claim to all of China including Mongolia. They have continued their government ever since, while the PRC has continued theirs on the mainland. The PRC meanwhile continues to claim Taiwan as a rebellious province of China, and has threatened military action against the island numerous times if it ever seeks greater international recognition. Neither the PRC nor the ROC recognize each other and both claim to be the sole legal representative of all of China. No peace treaty or armistice was ever signed between the two sides, so what lingers on between mainland China and Taiwan can almost be seen as a continuation of the Chinese Civil War that started over a century ago.

Today, the PRC refuses to have diplomatic relations with any country that officially recognizes the ROC. The small list of countries that continue to recognize the ROC and not the PRC include: Belize, Burkina Faso, the Dominican Republic, El Salvador, Guatemala, Haiti, Honduras, Kiribati, Marshall Islands, Nauru, Nicaragua, Palau, Panama,

Paraguay, Saint Kitts and Nevis, Saint Lucia, Saint Vincent and the Grenadines, Solomon Islands, Swaziland, Tuvalu, and Vatican City.

Every other country on earth besides the above choose to recognize the People's Republic of China instead, and have not officially recognized Taiwan or the ROC as an independent nation. The situation is so touchy that, even at the Olympics, Taiwan (ROC) must compete under the name of "Chinese Taipei" for all official events so as not to offend the People's Republic.

Did the Olympics Create More Countries?

Speaking of the Olympics—one might logically propose that as another alternative to determine how many countries exist in the world, right? Yet here again you'd be arriving at a weird and controversial conclusion.

Remember how earlier in the chapter I said that there are 193 official UN member states? Well, if you look at how many countries participated in the 2016 Summer Olympics in Brazil, you'll get an answer of 207 countries—fourteen more than supposedly exist at the UN.

What gives?

Who are these fourteen mysterious countries that compete in the Olympics but don't have a table at the UN? Well, Kosovo and Palestine both competed—which we've already discussed—and the ROC competed under the name of Chinese Taipei, which we've also established as an outlier in the count. All of that makes total sense so far, right?

Apparently, to inflate the numbers somewhat, several islands that happen to be part of other countries got the opportunity to compete as independent nations at the Olympics. Examples include: Aruba which is part of the

Netherlands; Bermuda, the Cayman Islands, Cook Islands, and the British Virgin Islands, which are all dependencies of the United Kingdom; and American Samoa, Guam, Puerto Rico, and the American Virgin Islands, which are all territories of the United States. For some reason, Hong Kong, a city in China, competed as an independent nation. Finally, there was a Refugee Team included among the list of "countries" participating in the event.

Why would the Olympics so readily inflate the number of countries participating? One can speculate that they are trying to make the Olympics appear larger and far grander than any other event. But even the Olympics sometimes has difficulty sorting out what should be considered an "independent country," as demonstrated in the following examples.

Countries You Probably Never Heard Of

Let's start off with one that is pretty obscure, though the territory is in plain sight: the Sahrawi Arab Democratic Republic. You may be familiar with this blank spot [graphic provided] on maps whenever you look at Africa. A reference often indicates something along the lines of "not sufficient data." When this area is referred to by the politically correct term "Western Sahara," no one becomes offended. However, things heat up when it is contentiously known as Morocco, the Sahrawi Arab Democratic Republic, or even Spanish Sahara.

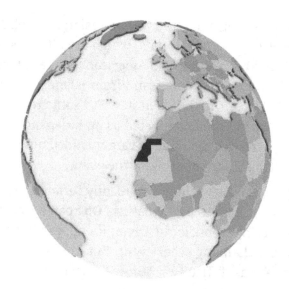

Western Sahara

The history behind this weird situation dates back to 1975. Back then, the territory was an overseas colony of Spain and known as Spanish Sahara. Under urging from the UN, Spain decided to give up this colony in 1975 and basically abandoned the area and left it for the people to figure it out for themselves. The area was claimed by multiple parties; the first of which, known as the Polisario Front, seeks to establish Western Sahara as a fully independent country.

The neighboring countries of Morocco and Mauritania also laid claims to the territory. Morocco invaded it while the Spanish were leaving and occupied the northern two thirds of the territory. Meanwhile, Mauritania occupied the lower third. The Polisario Front began a guerilla war against both the Moroccans and Mauritanians and gained support from Algeria. The fighting was too much for Mauritania, which withdrew its claim and pulled out in 1979. This encouraged Morocco to then claim *all* of Western Sahara as its own.

The Sahrawi Arab Democratic Republic was declared by the Polisario Front in 1976 with claims to all of Western Sahara as its core territory. The Polisario Front continued the guerilla war against Morocco until a ceasefire agreement was signed in 1991. This is where the situation stands today.

Morocco considers Western Sahara to be its "Southern Provinces," and currently occupies about 75 to 80 percent of the territory. The Sahrawi Arab Democratic Republic (SADR), meanwhile, occupies the remaining 20 to 25 percent, which you can see in the figure on the previous page. The current UN member states recognize the SADR, and the SADR is a full member of the African Union. The SADR is most heavily supported by Algeria. Morocco's claims to the entirety of Western Sahara are supported most heavily by the United States, France, and most of the Arab League.

Ever since 1975, there has been a planned referendum on whether this territory should become an independent country or join Morocco. To date, this has not occurred.

To some people, the Sahrawi Arab Democratic Republic is a full country, but to others it's simply a rebel group inside Morocco. This is a common theme we'll continue to see throughout the remainder of this chapter. Depending on who you ask, a territory may be either an independent country or a group of rebels that occupy part of a "real" country.

Other examples of this phenomenon include the Republic of Somaliland, which declared its independence from Somalia back in 1991. Thirty years earlier, Somaliland was briefly an independent country for five days when it gained independence from the United Kingdom. Shortly afterward, it joined Somalia. No country besides Somaliland itself recognizes it, and Somalia continues to claim it as part of its own territory. This defies logic when you consider that

Somaliland has its own government for its four million people, elects its own leaders, has its own currency, and maintains some trade relations with neighboring countries. All of that seems to fit our definition of what a country is, doesn't it?

So, how many countries in the world are we up to now— 206? 193? 195? 197?

The Nagorno-Karabakh Republic and the Pridnestrovian Moldovan Republic

Hold on: We aren't quite finished yet. We next have the category of non-UN member states that are recognized only by other non-UN member states. This elite group includes the "countries" of the Nagorno-Karabakh Republic and the Pridnestrovian Moldovan Republic.

The Nagorno-Karabakh Republic is awkward and has a lot of ugly history behind it. It is considered to be a part of Azerbaijan currently in the Caucuses, but the population of the Nagorno-Karabakh region is ethnically Armenian. Nearly a century ago in 1918, when the Ottoman Empire collapsed, Armenia and Azerbaijan both achieved independence. The two countries disputed the Nagorno-Karabakh region and fought a brief war over the territory in 1920.

However, the issue of who controlled it instantaneously became moot because the Soviet Union came in and took over both countries. The Soviets decided that Nagorno-Karabakh would be placed inside the Azerbaijan SSR instead of the Armenian SSR. Fast forward several decades to 1991 and the Soviet Union also collapsed, leaving Armenia and Azerbaijan independent once again.

Amidst the chaos, Nagorno-Karabakh held a referendum and declared its independence from Azerbaijan at almost the same time that Azerbaijan declared its own independence from the Soviet Union. Azerbaijan refused to recognize Nagorno-Karabakh's independence and responded with military force. Armenia, meanwhile, joined the war and sided with Nagorno-Karabakh. The war dragged on for several years with tens of thousands of deaths and ended in a stalemate.

Nagorno-Karabakh has been left in this awkward limbo ever since. The region is a part of Azerbaijan, but is de facto independent or even a part of Armenia. Yet nobody in the world recognizes it as such—except Abkhazia and South Ossetia, which we'll get to later—and Transnistria, which is our next discussion.

Is Transnistria a Country?

Transnistria, also known as the Pridnestrovian Moldovan Republic, is a thin strip of land that stretches about 250 miles north to south, but is no more than a mere 15 miles wide on average. The entire region is like a time capsule into the late 1980s Soviet Union; the flag still includes the Soviet hammer and sickle, statues of Lenin and Marx and can be found across the country, and streets are still proudly named after Communist philosophers and thinkers.

Today the area is home to slightly over a half million people and they have their own republic, government, parliament, military, police, postal system, currency, and even license plates. Seems exactly like a country—except for the fact that not a single UN country recognizes it as such. Instead, the world pretends that it's part of Moldova.

You may be wondering why this is the case. Well, once again it all started with the collapse of the Soviet Union in 1991. As in the case of Armenia and Azerbaijan, Moldova declared its independence from the USSR at that time. For the most part, the people of Moldova speak Romanian, and their new independence caused a surge of Moldovan nationalism in the country. Laws were passed that promoted the use of Romanian over other languages such as Russian, and that wasn't ever going to be popular in the region that would become Transnistria.

Transnistria wasn't, and isn't, like the rest of Moldova; her people primarily speak Russian, and they are kind of a melting pot of the former USSR. The populations of ethnic Russians, Moldovans, and Ukrainians in Transnistria are all almost equal—many of them having migrated to the area during the Soviet days. This population engaged in armed rebellion against the government of Moldova in 1992 out of nostalgia for the former Soviet Union. Their aim was to keep the Soviet Union alive, at least in their tiny pocket of the world.

Moldova

Are These On-Screen Countries Real?

If you are a fan of old film comedies, no doubt the Marx Brothers' *Duck Soup* tops your list. If you believe that Freedonia—the country ruled by Rufus T. Firefly (Groucho Marx) in the film—ever existed, you will be disappointed. The country is complete fiction, though the name has historic references. Right after the American Revolution, some Americans referred to themselves as "Freedonians" (which, needless to say, didn't stick). Briefly, between 1826–1827, a Texan rebel group referred to themselves as the "Republic of Fredonia." But that's pretty much the extent of it.

The "country" of San Marcos has also shown up in a classic movie comedy: Woody Allen's 1971 film *Bananas*. The banana republic of San Marcos never actually existed, but that didn't prevent it from also showing up on episodes of the television shows *MacGyver* and *Archer*.

Now, what about Kazakhstan? The country "documented" in Sacha Baron Cohen's satirical film *Borat*? Is that a country? The answer is "yes"—though the "mockumentary" butchered quite a few facts about the country for comic effect. Kazakhstan is actually the ninth largest landlocked country in the world and has a population of around eighteen million people. Contrary to depictions in the film, Kazakhstan is more tolerant than most Muslim nations when it comes to treatment of its Jewish population and even has relations with Israel. *Borat* was banned in Kazakhstan—even though it ironically led to a boon in the country's tourist industry. Poland, Romania, and Italy).

It wouldn't have gone anywhere had the Russian military not gotten involved on the side of Transnistria and forced Moldova into signing a ceasefire. Transnistria has remained a de facto independent country ever since, but without receiving the recognition of Russia—the country that fought in a war to help it secure some autonomy. Instead, Transnistria is only recognized by Nagorno-Karabakh (which we just previously discussed) and two other entities that may or may not be countries, depending upon whom you ask: Abkhazia and South Ossetia.

Is South Ossetia a Country?

Let's begin with South Ossetia, which declared its independence from the country of Georgia in 1991 (yes, you guessed it, again from the Soviet Union). Georgia is located in the Caucasus Mountains between Russia to the north and Turkey to the southwest. South Ossetia, meanwhile, is sandwiched between the north of Georgia and Russia. The territory has a population of 53,000 people and takes up an area larger than the country of Luxembourg. The territory is also home to a defined group of people, the Ossetians. The historical region of "Ossetia" is currently divided between Russia and Georgia, with North Ossetia being located inside Russia and South Ossetia being located inside Georgia. With all of this in mind (if you are capable of holding on to all of this mind-boggling detail), South Ossetia declared its independence from Georgia in 1991 with two goals in mind: first, to create an independent Ossetian state; and, secondly, to possibly join the Russian Federation and unite with North Ossetia, which is already a part of Russia.

Georgia responded with military force against the South Ossetian Declaration of Independence and started a civil war inside the country that lasted between 1991 and 1992. Russia brokered a ceasefire agreement between the two sides and hostilities somewhat died down until they resurfaced in 2004 and again in 2008.

The 2008 conflict was more significant because Russia decided to actually intervene with its own military against

Georgia. The 2008 Russo-Georgian War is considered by many to be the first European War of the twenty-first century. In August of that year, Russia launched a full-scale invasion of Georgia and blockaded her coast. Russia won the war in a matter of days, which led to the awkward situation today, in which South Ossetia is a de facto independent country inside Georgia that is officially recognized by the governments of Russia, Nicaragua, Venezuela, and Nauru—which are all official UN member states. All of these countries also recognize Abkhazia as a fully independent country, which is also a breakaway part of Georgia.

The 2008 Russo-Georgian War also established Abkhazia as a full de facto independent country inside Georgia, despite having limited international recognition outside of Russia. Abkhazia is located a little further northwest of South Ossetia and is also sandwiched between Russia and Georgia, but has a coast along the Black Sea. The territory is much larger than South Ossetia—taking up an area a little smaller than Puerto Rico—and is home to around 243,000 people.

The region fought against Georgia in 1992 and, by the following year, Abkhazia emerged as a de facto independent nation but without any international recognition. During the 2008 Russo-Georgian War, Abkhazia entered on the side of Russia and South Ossetia and attacked Georgia. This led to the Russian government formally recognizing Abkhazia as an independent country, along with the other ones that recognized South Ossetia.

Break Time: Our Current Tally of Countries

Since it's likely you are lost in figuring the number of countries by now, I think it's time for a review of where we stand with the tally. Keep in mind that I am not advocating

inclusion or non-inclusion of any of these countries:
Like you, I just want a straight answer about how many
countries there are in the world. If an alien species were
to descend to our planet in a space ship, make peaceful
introductions, and ask how many countries we have, what
would we answer? Why must it be so difficult?

We began with the number 195 because that's how many
countries are technically present at the United Nations.
Adding Vatican City increases it to 196. Then we subtracted
Palestine and The Holy See because technically they are UN
observers and not official UN member states. This brings us
to 194.

But wait. If 70 percent of countries in the world
recognize Palestine as an official country, shouldn't the
answer once again be 195? If that isn't enough to make your
head swirl, remember that there are thirty-one UN member
states that don't recognize Israel as an official country.
However, many of those do recognize Palestine, so the
answer would go back down to 194.

We also have the case of Kosovo, which is officially
recognized by 110 UN member countries—but not by the
other eighty-three member states. The number could be 194
or 195, depending on whom you ask. Now let's say that you
consider all of these places to be countries: Palestine, Israel,
Kosovo, and Vatican City. What number would we have then?
One hundred and 97, of course, but as you know, we've come
up with additional countries to factor into the equation.

If we were to include the ROC (a.k.a. Taiwan) to the list,
then our number is raised to 198. If you go by the number of
countries participating in the Olympics, then it increases the
answer to 207 because it includes all of the countries that
we've discussed in this paragraph and the last one, minus

Vatican City. As you'll recall, the 207 figure includes Puerto Rico, Guam, and the Virgin Islands, which make no claims to independence—so that definition is kind of nebulous.

Guess what—we are now we're back to 198...but, if we're including Taiwan and Kosovo, then we should probably include the other limited recognition states we've mentioned: the Sahrawi Arab Democratic Republic (recognized by eighty-four UN member states) and the Republics of South Ossetia and Abkhazia (which are both recognized by four UN member states).

That gives us 201 as the answer...but what about the places we discussed that don't without any official UN member recognition: Somaliland, Nagorno-Karabakh, and Transnistria. If we include all three of those, our answer suddenly becomes 204.

Wait. I can't believe I'm doing this to you (and myself): We still have a few more places/countries to go. I just wanted to catch you up to where we currently are in the count. We're almost done, I promise!

Cyprus: It's Not All Greek to Me

Map of Cyprus

Located in the Eastern Mediterranean, Cyprus is the third biggest island in the Mediterranean Sea. Though there were early settlers, the first documented control of Cyprus dates back to the Mycenaean Greeks in the second millennium BCE.

Over the centuries, Cyprus has been inhabited by many different groups. For most of recent history, it's been ruled by two main ethnic groups: the Greeks and the Turks.

Let's attempt to sum up hundreds of years of history in one paragraph. Cyprus was part of the Ottoman Empire from the sixteenth to the latter part of the nineteenth century, but then the British took it over. Greece and Turkey became enraged because nobody residing on the island was actually English. The British decided to not make it their problem anymore by letting Cyprus ~~become independent~~ make up its own mind. It seemed as if Cyprus was going to join Greece because a majority of the island's population was Greek. The deal was imminent when Turkey became upset by the decision and invaded the island. Turkey conquered about one third of the island before a UN ceasefire went into effect that ended hostilities. The only problem was that Turkey decided to stay. Rather than fold their third of Cyprus in their country, Turkey instead created a new country called "The Turkish Republic of Northern Cyprus."

This de facto independent country continues to exist on the island of Cyprus along with the other country, "The Republic of Cyprus." The international community overwhelmingly rejects the Turkish Republic of Northern Cyprus as a country; they insist that all of Cyprus belongs to the Republic of Cyprus, which gained independence from the United Kingdom. The only UN member country in the world that recognizes the Turkish Republic of Northern Cyprus is...well, you probably already guessed it, Turkey. So, according to the Turkish government, the number of countries is now probably 205; however, according to the rest of the world, it's still 204.

The Korean Conundrum

It's inevitable that at some point we must address the Korean peninsula, which is currently occupied by two different UN member countries: South Korea and North Korea, also known respectively as the "Republic of Korea" and the "People's Democratic Republic of Korea." Surprise! Both countries refuse to recognize each other as a legitimate country. Both claim the entirety of the Korean peninsula as theirs. North Korea believes that all of South Korea is rightfully theirs, and vice versa. If you were to ask either North Korea or South Korea how many countries exist in the world, the answer might be the same—203—since neither side recognizes the other.

One Final Consideration: Armenia

I promise, you are just about at the end of this nightmare question with one last (but not least) area to consider: Armenia.

Armenia certainly meets every criterion of being a country and is an official member of the United Nations, but that hasn't stopped a country located over 1,000 miles away from thinking otherwise: Pakistan. This country continues to support Azerbaijan because of the previously mentioned Nagorno-Karabakh War between Azerbaijan and Armenia. In a show of support for Azerbaijan, Pakistan refuses to recognize Armenia as a country—which is perplexing, because even *Azerbaijan* recognizes Armenia, as does every other UN member country in the world. In any event, according to Pakistan, the answer would also be 203—like the Koreas—but for a different reason.

Armenia

In Summary: Make Up Your Own Mind

To condense this admittedly lengthy chapter into an explicit answer: There is no consensus on how many countries exist in the world. I'm sorry. The answer is completely dependent on whom you're talking to or your personal beliefs. Do you think Transnistria, Abkhazia, or South Ossetia are really countries? Are the Olympics correct in claiming Puerto Rico and Guam as countries? Perhaps one of the two Koreas isn't actually a real country? (Let's not start a war here on that!) Everybody has a different answer to the same question, but every answer has one thing in common: They're all generally pretty close to the number 200. So, let's just say *around 200* and leave it at that.

Of course, you could tilt that to *over 200* by creating a country of your own. After you answer the following trivia questions, flip to the next chapter and find out if you have what it takes to do it.

HOW MUCH DO YOU KNOW ABOUT COUNTRIES?

1. Is Kiribati a real country?

2. Is Klaatu a real country?

3. What country covers the most time zones?

4. What country cited in this chapter has the most 7-Eleven convenience stores per person than any other?

5. What nationality is Sacha Baron Cohen? (Hint: He's *not* from Kazakhstan.)

CHAPTER FIVE

A TUTORIAL ON CREATING YOUR OWN COUNTRY

If a nation expects to be ignorant and free, in a state of civilization, it expects what never was and never will be.

—Thomas Jefferson

Now that you know how many countries there are—or at least have an understanding of all the perspectives on the matter—perhaps you believe you can do a better job than the people running them and have an itch to start your own independent country. Is it even possible for one person to accomplish such a thing? How do countries come into existence in the first place?

The answer to the first question is absolutely yes: Theoretically, it is entirely possible for you to create your own country at this very moment. The answer to the second question is complicated, and may make the answer to the first question a bit problematic.

As mentioned earlier in this book, the declarative theory of statehood outlines a somewhat commonly accepted definition of "what is a country." Signed back in 1933, the theory—which we'll review again—outlines the criteria for determining which places are countries and which ones are not.

The state as a person of international law should possess the following qualifications:

- A permanent population
- A defined territory
- A government
- A capacity to enter into relations with other states

The first sentence of article three is somewhat surprising: "The political existence of the state is independent of recognition by the other states." This conflicts with the opposing Constitutive Theory of Statehood, which asserts that international recognition by other states is vital to the existence of a country. So, which is it?

Let's make it easier on ourselves by pushing that niggling contradiction aside. Instead, we may begin by figuring out how to clear the first four bullet points above to meet the criteria of the declarative theory of statehood. Then we'll figure out how you can get the international recognition demanded by the constitutive theory of statehood.

This Land Is Your Land

What would you guess is the first thing you need in order to start a country? Territory, of course.

But what if you don't have any territory to claim? Believe it or not, this is not an insurmountable problem. You can get around it by claiming your country is a part of another country that is currently being occupied. But claiming your country is part of another one is not as simple as sticking a two-sided flag (one side bearing your country's emblem and the other the American flag) on your patio deck.

If I were to step into my backyard and declare it the newfound country of *RealLifeLore* Land, for example, I could genuinely believe that it was a real independent country. The problem here is that the prevailing authorities—the city government, the county government, the state government, and the federal government—would all severely disagree with and dispute my claims. My property would still be subject to property tax and, if I refused to pay it because I claimed that my backyard was an "independent country," well...bad things would happen. Sooner or later my house and property would get foreclosed and be sold to somebody else. If I refuse I could end up involved in an armed standoff.

You may be thinking the government of a "foreign power" declared war on me in the above scenario, but this is a useless argument. They would eventually win and confiscate my territory. My bid to create an independent country would fail miserably. No wonder more people don't start their own countries—it's not so easy!

Hail, Hail Molossia!

Another way to go about creating a country is to start a *micronation*, which means what it sounds like: *a small country*. A micronation is essentially when you create your own country but no governing body or organization recognizes you as such.

The most well known micronation in the United States is Molossia—no, I didn't make this up—located in Dayton, Nevada. Suffice to say, it has not been accepted by the United Nations—nor does it have an Olympic team. However, it does have its own currency, runs its own post office, and even has something of a "space program."

Molossia was founded in 1999 by a retired army sergeant named Kevin Baugh. His full title is—brace yourself for this—Excellency President Grand Admiral Colonel Doctor Kevin Baugh, President and Raïs of Molossia, Protector of the Nation and Guardian of the People.

His Excellency Baugh, the "benevolent dictator," rules over two pieces of land comprising about 6.3 square acres and a citizenry of thirty-three people (counting his family... and some dogs). If you wish to visit, you are more than welcome to see fascinating sights such as the cemetery, the library, the store, and the decorative tower—but be mindful that in order to enter you must go through the strict "border patrol" to have your passport stamped.

Two major upsides to Molossia: they do continue to pay taxes to the US Government; and they have never gone to war. On the other hand, their national anthem is a rip-off of the Albanian National Anthem—with amended lyrics, of course.

We've only just begun and have already hit a roadblock. Where can we find territory that isn't actually a part of an already existing country? Is there even any land left on this planet that doesn't already belong to somebody else? The answer is...yes!

Under international law, unclaimed land is known as *terra nullius*. This is territory that has never been subject to the sovereignty of any state—or it is territory for which prior ownership claims have been relinquished. Sovereignty over terra nullius territory can be established simply by occupying it. However, this can be quite difficult logistically and would still present numerous headaches.

There are few places in the world today that are considered terra nullius. One such area, known as Bir Tawil, is located between Egypt and Sudan. It's actually quite a large piece of land at 2,060 square kilometers (800 square miles) in size, which is almost the same as Luxembourg (2,586 square kilometers, 998 square miles).

The situation first arose as a political dispute between the neighboring countries of Egypt and Sudan. A straight political border was established in 1899 between the two countries, but an irregular administrative border was created in 1902. You can see the borders in the diagram with Bir Tawil situated between them.

Also in the middle of these borders is another piece of land further to the east, known as the Hala'ib Triangle. This territory is considered even more valuable than Bir Tawil. Egypt asserts the 1899 straight political border, while Sudan asserts the 1902 irregular administrative border. The 1899 political border would place the Hala'ib Triangle within Egypt, but Bir Tawil in Sudan. Meanwhile, the 1902 border would place the Hala'ib Triangle within Sudan and Bir Tawil in Egypt.

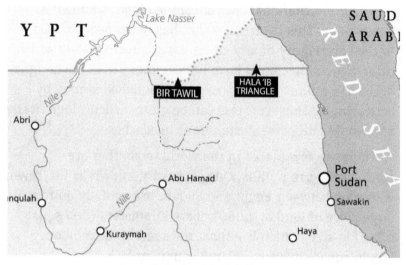

Bir Tawil and the Hala 'Ib

Confused enough yet? Neither country has a basis under international law to possess the territories, so they both claim the much more valuable Hala'ib Triangle and refuse Bir Tawil. Egypt arguably administers the area, but Bir Tawil is not marked as part of Egypt on any Egyptian maps. Since Bir Tawil is landlocked and located right in the center of Egypt and Sudan, no other country in the world has ever laid claim to it. Thus, Bir Tawil has been described by some as the only habitable place on Earth unclaimed by any recognized government.

With this in mind, what's stopping you from closing this book right now and plotting out a land grab? You could book a flight to Cairo or Khartoum and travel across the desert to Bir Tawil, where you would then plant a flag on a hilltop to proclaim your new country. What's to stop you?

A few things might get in your way, but technically they're all manageable. Sort of. The first issue to consider is the extremely harsh climate of Bir Tawil. It is, after all, located in the middle of the Sahara Desert. You'd need a strong camel, lots of bottled water, and a significant amount of sunscreen and deodorant.

Unlike Las Vegas, another desert, Bir Tawil doesn't have any hotels from which to choose accommodations. There aren't any real bathrooms or stores, just sand, and has a teeny tiny population (well, zero when last reported in 2014). You would be completely on your own while staking your flag in the ground in unbearable dry heat—and undoubtedly without a wireless signal.

Let's pretend you could accomplish all of the above and survive. You would have made up a country name, a flag design, an anthem, and maybe even some currency. Congratulations! You have reached the 25 percent mark in creating your country!

A Country Needs People

Hold on a minute, Amerigo. Before you get cocky, remember that another important criteria for creating a country is that you must have a population. It goes without saying one person doesn't make a census. In fact, you need to have a *permanent population* within your defined territory. You're living in Bir Tawil all alone—so how do you attract other people to come and join you there? How do you make an empty desert attractive to potential homesteaders, a.k.a. new countrymen?

Here's an idea: You could start a cult or found a new religion. This sounds pretty far-fetched and insane, but hear me out and roll with it. You could advertise that Bir Tawil as some sort of holy land or a place where your newfound faith could seek refuge from the rest of the world. This is not as outlandish as it sounds. These scenarios have happened numerous times in history. Consider examples like the Puritans coming to the New World or the Mormons venturing across America to modern day Utah.

Jumping ahead, let's assume that you've managed to accumulate a large following of converts to your religious order. You've convinced your flock that Bir Tawil is some kind of promised land—a feat numerous prophets and charismatic individuals have accomplished in the past elsewhere. Your people follow you all of the way across the desert, break ceremonial first ground, and settle there. They build homes, a school, a church and, most importantly, a Starbucks. Now you are in business, having fulfilled the criteria of a permanent population.

If you went the religious group/cult route, you could probably create some kind of weird theocracy in the middle of the desert that's built around whatever your group chooses to believe in.

All right, it's possible you are entirely repulsed by the whole "start a cult/religion" thing. You could name yourself as the entire permanent population. I admit it, I misled you a bit on purpose. The requirements say nothing about *how many people* must be a part of the permanent population. One individual person is still a population, isn't it? And, if you are living in your territory permanently, then you would still count as fulfilling that requirement. Hooray!

Government for the People (or Person)

With your permanent population of one firmly established, you then need to turn to the next order of business: creation of an actual *government*. In order to attract people to move to the area of their own free will and without the need to resort to religious charlatanism, you should probably either be: (1) rich enough to pay them generous grants as an incentive or (2) capable of creating a type of government that would attract people to the area.

Types of Oddball Governments to Consider for Your Country

There have been many types of government created around the world over the years—some stranger than others. *Anarchy* is often the one that comes to mind most because people think there is nothing to it except "pure chaos." This couldn't be further from what true anarchists believe. Philosophically, they feel there is governmental order but that no one may be forced into doing things they don't want to do (such as submitting to a forced draft).

If you happen to possess a genius IQ, then a *geniocracy* type of government might be right for you. The brainchild of a former racecar driver named Claude Maurice Marcel Vorilhon who changed his name to Raël, founded geniocracy as a government in which only smart people have governmental rights. You may vote if your IQ is 110 or above, but you can only hold office at 150 or higher.

Some of you probably find the above to be pretty discriminatory against those of lesser intelligence, so you might want to try to establish a *plutarchy* instead. Economist Robin Hanson conceived this type of government, which he explains as follows: "We would vote on values, but bet on beliefs." In other words, all legislative decisions rest on assigned market speculators determining which proposed policies would most benefit the national welfare.

These three options might not be so bad when you compare them with how most dictatorships and monarchies turned out over the centuries.

Since it's unlikely you have millions of dollars to spend on bribing people to immigrate to your country, you probably want to go down the path of number two: Establish a government that will lure people in.

This most effective option is relatively easy, although you may consider it morally reprehensible: create a tax haven! Trust me when I state that if your government has zero tax laws or extremely lax tax laws, you will get significant interest.

In this scenario, you would allow anybody to move into your country with the understanding that income tax would not be applied to them. You would then need to seek out investors to build projects in the country. You would give away real estate within the territory for free. Minimum wage would not exist (or it would be minimal), so you can undercut any third-world developing country in the world. Here is the biggie to bring in corporations: You would promise them almost no tax, no regulations, and a free rein allowing them to handle their businesses however they see fit (e.g., including cheap but immoral practices, such as child labor). In a nutshell, you would be turning your little piece of land into a total libertarian and capitalist "paradise."

There are some other tricky issues to figure out with your new country based in Bir Tawil. As previously mentioned, it is landlocked so you would need to find a way to build an airport, or corporations would have no ability to transport anyone or anything there.

I admit I don't know how you would even begin to build an airport in the middle of a desert. Likely you would have to make an investment in hiring some world-class engineers.

There is a second challenge that's pretty daunting: How do you recruit a work force in one of the worst environments in the world? I suppose if you were a huge bastard and didn't care at all about morals or human rights, you could go down the cult route and use masses of gullible religious-minded people as your unwitting labor force once you attract capitalists to the area.

When it comes to fanatics, however, there is high risk that exploiting them would lead to dissent and eventually an outright revolt. This could only be suppressed if you had the backing of some kind of loyal police force behind you.

Recruitment to build your police force and army wouldn't be quite as difficult as some of the other challenges faced in creating a country. You would hand-select the strongest, fiercest, and most dedicated cult/religion members. They would remain loyal if you pay them well and give them lots of fun, destructive weapons to play with.

Infrastructure Is Critical

Infrastructure is critical to the success of your nation and in gaining future investments and attracting businesses. Your only option is to devote all government to funding land development. You would need to be absolutely heartless, sparing no money for basic health care, education, and community programs. Rather, all government resources would be invested in areas essential to support business: the development of roads, buildings, water aquifers, and power plants. The promises of a cheap and exploitable labor force, coupled with no income tax, would entice myriad companies to build their factories in your country.

Most factories require a great deal of energy in order to produce goods. If you build enough power plants to supply what is needed to sustain these factories, you will do well. Since Bir Tawil is in the Sahara Desert and gets a lot of sun, perhaps your most sensible energy option is to construct vast arrays of solar panels.

Maintaining Your Work Force

Maintaining a work force in the middle of the desert is not an easy matter, especially if you exploit them to maximum capacity. Eventually, they will grow tired and sick. As you'll recall, you are grudging with health care in your country so it's likely many will become too ill to work or will drop dead without proper treatment. How can you keep the workforce of your brand new country going if you don't have an able-bodied workforce?

Quite simply, you will need to recruit a new workforce to replace the old. Assuming once again you have a complete lack of empathy and zero morals, you could trick people into coming into the territory with the false hopes of rewarding work. Or, you could kidnap them and smuggle them in using additional unsavory tactics.

A practical idea would be to centralize your factory hub and operations center in the middle of the country. This way, a rebellious workforce desperate to escape would have no place to run. Your country is underdeveloped and situated in the middle of a desert. It's not like there are any roads or signs directing people where to go. There wouldn't be any water or food for survival. The journey to the next nearest country is hundreds of kilometers/miles away, which they would have to traverse by foot on sand in blistering heat.

Then there is the matter of what happens when they reach one of the neighboring countries, Egypt or Sudan; both also have harsh desert-like climates. The area around Bir Tawil is remote in both countries, so if an escaped worker were to make it that far he would have a difficult time finding the nearest help. That's not even taking into account that your loyal police officers or soldiers might them hunt down and capture them. But, you wouldn't want to kill them, because you need as many workers alive as possible. Shooting down employees might deter some capitalists from setting up shop in your country or doing business with you. Word might also get around that you aren't exactly a lenient boss and future employee recruitment might be all the more challenging.

So, Do You Have What It Takes?

All of this obviously assumes you are soulless. You would be something of a monster to go down this route in order to be successful creating your own country in the middle of the desert by yourself.

Before you dismiss this completely, though, ask yourself the following honest question: How exactly do you think every country in history got started? This question may trouble you for some time. The fact of the matter is that the founding of a country has never been a peaceful endeavor and almost always involves the exploitation of some kind of group. As nightmarish as this scenario might seem, keep in mind the current and past histories of real countries, movements, cults, and other ideologies. I am almost certain that you found some comparison with real circumstances while having read this chapter.

Now for the most important question of all: What will you *name* your country? Sorry, you are on your own with that—and Canada has already been taken.

HOW MUCH DO YOU KNOW ABOUT COUNTRIES?

1. Which country or countries have avoided war
    the longest?

2. Among the following country names, which one
    is a real country: Footland, Abhazia, West Korea,
    The Republic of Nebraska, Provinstan, or Druidia.

3. Among the following country names, which one has
    never been considered a real country: Kyrgyzstan,
    Comoros, Malawi, Kataan, or Vanuatu.

4. Which actor from this list is the only one born in the
    United States: Charlize Theron, Scarlett Johansson,
    Keanu Reeves, Ryan Gosling, or Anna Paquin.

5. How many (legitimate) countries does the Sahara
    Desert span?

CHAPTER SIX

PRESIDENTS, POLITICS, AND THE NUCLEAR FOOTBALL

*When I was in the White House, I was confronted with
the challenge of the Cold War. Both the Soviet Union and
I had 30,000 nuclear weapons that could destroy the entire
Earth and I had to maintain the peace.*

—Jimmy Carter

The President of the United States is accompanied wherever he goes at all times by a military aide who carries "the football." Is this so the President can break out into a pick-up two-hand touch game with the Secret Service and his aides whenever he's in the mood for exercise?

Not exactly. The football—which is referred to by a number of various names, including "the nuclear football," the "atomic football," the "President's emergency satchel," the "Presidential emergency satchel," the "black box," or "the button"—is the briefcase that contains the devices needed in order for the President to authorize a nuclear attack.

The President of the United States is the only person who has the authority to order a nuclear strike. The President always carries a plastic card on his person known as "the biscuit" that contains verification codes needed to authorize a strike using the football.

The Nuclear Football

How Is Nuclear Football Played?

The National Security Agency (NSA) creates a new card with unique codes every single day to be available for the President to use, if he deems it necessary. The card is also printed with numerous fake codes that are meaningless; the President must memorize which part of the codes printed on the card are the actual codes. Should the President decide to order the launch of nuclear weapons, he would be taken aside by the carrier of the football. The briefcase would be opened and the President would decide on a plan.

Inside the briefcase is a black book that contains preset war plans and strike locations around the world, which can range from a single cruise missile strike to the complete launch of all of America's thousands of nuclear weapons. In addition to the black book, there is a folder that gives protocol for the emergency alert system. There is another book with top-secret locations located across the US where the President and his staff could be taken in an emergency and from where they may continue to run the US government safely in the event of a retaliatory strike.

Once the President has selected a particular war plan, the aide would use the communication technology in the football to make contact with the National Military Command Center and/or multiple airborne command posts and nuclear-armed submarines.

The One Safety Net

While the President is the only individual with the authority to order the use of nuclear weapons, there is one legal check before the nuclear bombs are launched. The Secretary of Defense must also approve and authenticate the President's commands in order for them to go through. However, the Secretary of Defense's role is *only to authenticate that the orders have truly come from the President.* Once the Secretary of Defense has confirmed this, legally he *must* approve of the President's orders; he has no veto or legal power whatsoever to reject the order.

In essence, the President does have the sole power to decide upon and order the use of nuclear weapons. Once the decision has been made, there isn't anything anybody can do short of an outright mutiny to stop him or her from firing the weapons. After the Secretary of Defense has authenticated that it was the President who gave the orders, the commands are sent to the Chairman of the Joint Chiefs of Staff, who then orders the military to carry out the President's plan.

What If the President Were to Go Cuckoo?

There is something of a failsafe in the Constitution in case the President goes off his rocker and decides to toss the nuclear football just for kicks. Section four of the twenty-fifth amendment to the United States Constitution allows for the Vice President—together with either a majority of the President's Cabinet or Congress—to declare the President disabled or unfit to execute the duties of office. The issue is that this takes a lot of time to accomplish—especially getting a majority of Congress to agree; meanwhile, the President can order a nuclear strike using the football in under fifteen minutes.

There are no other safeguards in place to verify that the person giving the order is "sane." Whoever the President is, his command must legally be followed. This is part of the reason why the President of the United States is considered the most powerful person in the world. Right at his fingertips, the President has the power to destroy entire countries, kill millions (if not *billions*) of people, and perhaps even annihilate the entire world—yet there are no real checks in place to Presidential power whatsoever when it comes to the nuclear football. Theoretically, he can decide to do this anytime he chooses.

Dr. Strangelove: Drama or Satire?

The 1964 Stanley Kubrick film *Dr. Strangelove or: How I Learned to Stop Worrying and Love the Bomb*, released during the height of the Cold War, depicted what might happen if a lunatic general were to go rogue and launch a nuclear air strike. Screenwriter Terry Southern adapted the screenplay from the novel, *Red Alert*, by Peter George. Somewhere along the adaptation process, Kubrick and Southern turned the serious doomsday novel into a comic satire. The main alteration? The character of Dr. Strangelove (portrayed by Peter Sellers) doesn't even appear in the book.

Discarded Defensive Nuclear Plays

There were two interesting ideas proposed during the Cold War to mitigate the potential risk of using nuclear weapons. Neither involved usage of the nuclear football.

The first might strike some people as a bit extreme. One brave individual would volunteer to have the nuclear codes implanted into his chest cavity near the heart. This individual would follow the President everywhere he went. Should the President ever decide to use nuclear weapons, he would have to physically take this volunteer's life by having him cut open for the codes. This would make the decision far more difficult for the President and might help ensure it was indeed a "do or die" situation for the nuclear football to be set in motion.

The second idea was a political twist involving something of a Yankee/Commie swap. A member of the President's close family would be sent to Moscow as a sort of hostage, while a member of the Soviet leader's family would be sent to Washington. This way, if either party ordered a strike on the other he would knowingly be killing a close family member, in addition to the millions of other lives.

What Happens If the Quarterback Ends Up on the Disabled List?

You should now have a full understanding of the President's responsibilities with the nuclear football. But what happens if the President is disabled or killed in a crisis? What is the succession plan for the nuclear football?

The Vice President has a separate nuclear football—replete with "biscuit" card and launch codes—that follows him or her around. However, this nuclear football remains inactive while the President is in command. The Vice

President is not in any way able to order a nuclear launch while the President is still alive or in office because the Secretary of Defense must first verify the orders as coming only from the President.

If the President is disabled and unable to perform his duties, the Vice President may propose to the Cabinet or Congress that the President be removed from office. In this event, it takes time for the votes to be cast and a decision to be made. If the majority of the Cabinet or Congress agree with the Vice President's claim, succession takes place and the nuclear football is handed to him or her.

However, if the President is killed, the rules of succession automatically apply and the Vice President gets sworn in as President as soon as possible. Once this occurs, the Vice President has the right to order the use of nuclear weapons with the approval of the Secretary of Defense with the same authority as his predecessor.

Contrary to what most people believe, there is no "rule" or "law" stating the President and Vice President can't travel together. It happens that they never do primarily because of scheduling issues; it's also a smart safety protocol.

In the highly unlikely event a huge catastrophe occurs in which both the President and Vice President are killed, here is the order of succession—and who would then be in a position to order the nuclear strikes:

1. Speaker of the House (leader of the House of Representatives)

2. President Pro Tempore of the Senate (most senior US Senator, longest serving Senator of the majority party)

3. Secretary of State

4. Secretary of the Treasury

5. Secretary of Defense

6. Attorney General

7. Secretary of the Interior

8. Secretary of Agriculture

9. Secretary of Commerce

10. Secretary of Labor

11. Secretary of Health and Human Services

12. Secretary of Housing and Urban Development

13. Secretary of Energy

14. Secretary of Education

15. Secretary of Veterans Affairs

16. Secretary of Homeland Security

There are numerous issues with this succession list. The first is that all of these people work in and reside near Washington D.C., which means that if a nuclear strike were to occur it is possible that all of these people would be killed. It's not really clear who would become President if all seventeen of these people, in addition to the President, were killed at the same time. It also makes one wonder what would happen to the nuclear launch codes. The line of succession could also awkwardly force the Presidency to abruptly switch party's mid-term, as the President, Speaker, and President pro tempore may not be of the same party.

For the time being, let's set our minds at ease that these situations will never occur and move onto other matters. The odds of losing so many high-ranking officials in the line of succession for the nuclear football all at once are astronomical. Then again, the odds have been of no consequence before—at least in the gamer of real life football. In the 2017 Super Bowl, the New England Patriots came back from a twenty-five-point deficit to defeat the Atlanta Falcons in overtime....

HOW MUCH DO YOU KNOW ABOUT PRESIDENTS, POLITICS, AND THE NUCLEAR FOOTBALL?

1. Who was the first President to have the nuclear football by his side?

2. What does the Secretary of the Interior actually do?

3. How many parts does British actor/comedian Peter Sellers play in *Dr. Strangelove*?

4. Which Presidents have owned football teams?

5. Does Vladimir Putin have a comparable nuclear football?

CHAPTER SEVEN

WHY IS MONEY BACKED BY GOLD?

Gold gets dug out of the ground in Africa, or someplace. Then we melt it down, dig another hole, bury it again, and pay people to stand around guarding it. It has no utility. Anyone watching from Mars would be scratching their head.

—Warren Buffett

Before we start looking at why gold is considered in such high regard, we probably need to have an understanding of money itself. What is money—aside from a way for us to purchase the things we need (food, clothing, shelter) and want (expensive jewelry, fancy cars, jet planes)?

Most economists state that money may be defined as two things: a store of value; and a unit of account. Before money was a real thing, everybody relied heavily on the barter system in which the only way to acquire goods and services was by trading goods and services.

Here is an easy example of the barter system in motion. Let's say that I have two shovels. I only need to use one, but what I really need is an ox to drag my cart. I must find someone who would be willing to trade an ox for my extra shovel. The problem with this method of economy is obvious almost immediately: What if I can't find a person who (a) has an ox (b) is in need of a shovel and (c) is willing trade his ox for the shovel. What if the one villager who owns an extra ox has no need for my shovel? Or, maybe the individual with the ox doesn't believe my shovel is worth the value of his ox? It's possible I have nothing of value that can entice him to trade away his ox.

This barter system relied upon something known as the *coincidence of wants.* You can only trade or barter for something if there happens to be a coincidence that two people need or want something from each other that they feel is of equal value. In other words, you both must have something that the other needs or wants. People often use clichés such as "money is evil" or "money is the root of all evil." But, the simple truth is that the world would be a much worse and far more confusing place than it currently is without money.

Gold Bars

Who Created the First Forms of Money?

Sorry—the specific answer to this question has not yet been pinpointed. However, it is known that the first metal objects serving as coins started to appear around 5,000 BCE. The Lydians (a people who settled in Anatolia, which is located in modern Turkey) started manufacturing coins around 700 BCE. Paper money originated in China in around 740 BCE.

Though forbidden by the British at the time, the first coins in the United States were created in 1652 by the Massachusetts Bay Colony. The colony printed the first paper money in 1690.

The United States minted its first coin (a half disme, pronounced like "dime") in 1792 and, in 1861, printed its first paper money as a means to finance Civil War efforts.

Money solved the coincidence of wants and the barter economy. If you create and assign something as a currency and then everybody recognizes it as being equally valuable, then you no longer need to have to worry about the availability or equality in the value of goods, property, or services to exchange. In the above example, the guy who didn't want my shovel might be fine instead with cash for his ox. I could sell my extra shovel for the right price to somebody who doesn't have an ox but needs this farming implement. Win–win!

How Did Gold Become So Valuable?

Now that we have established the need for money and how it replaced the flawed barter system, we can address the matter of gold. Namely, we want to reveal how and why gold not only became a currency itself, but also how it became a *backer* of currency. And finally, how and why did most modern economies leave the gold standard for fiat-based currency systems?

Over the years, there have been many forms of currency, in addition to metal coinage and paper money. This incredibly interesting list includes:

- Giant stones (Rai stones)

- Salt (in ancient Rome, the word "salary" derives from the Latin word *salarium*—which is Latin for salt)

- Candy (which was used as a currency in some parts of Argentina after the 2008 financial crisis)

- Pepper (it is alleged that in 408 AD Attila the Hun demanded a ransom of 3,000 pounds of pepper in exchange for not destroying the city of Rome)

- Beaver pelts (used as a common currency in colonial America, as they were valued by both Native Americans and colonists)

- Cocaine (sometimes used as a currency in remote or rural parts of Colombia even today)

- Buckskins (used as a common form of currency in colonial America; these pelts were taken from bucks in the wild. It is believed that the slang word "buck" for a dollar originates with this practice)

- Whale teeth (was used as a form of currency across many islands in the Pacific, especially around the islands of Fiji)

When you think about it, anything can be used as a form of currency as long as all parties involved agree on its value and worth. So why is it that throughout human history gold has been almost universally accepted as extremely valuable? Cultures and civilizations from all around the world at different times in history have considered gold to be precious: the Egyptians, Hittites, Romans, Huns, Chinese, Indian civilizations, Mali, African kingdoms, European colonial powers, Aztecs, and the Mayans. Just about every single civilization in history has used gold as a currency or currency backer and the question remains: why and how? Could it just be human nature to regard gold as valuable simply because it is shiny and pretty?

For starters, gold really is quite rare. If you were to take all of the gold that has ever been mined and then smelted it down to form a solid gold cube, how big do you think it would be? You are probably visualizing something gigantic when in reality the cube would merely have equal sides of about 21 meters long. That doesn't seem terribly large as the sum total of *all* of the world's gold supply. You can imagine how a 21 meter cube divided among the world's population of 7.5 billion people makes gold a rare commodity indeed. Scarcity is therefore one of the primary historical reasons for gold's value.

Supply and Demand

Most of you are probably familiar with the law of supply and demand. It is a core component of economic thought and essentially states the following: Any commodity that has high demand but low supply will be expensive or costly because there simply isn't enough of it for everybody. Only the people willing to pay a lot for the commodity will attain it over the people unwilling or unable to pay that price.

Alternatively, any commodity with low demand but high supply will be relatively cheap because, while there is a lot of the item, not a lot of people want it. To entice people to buy up the large supply, the owner of that supply reduces his or her prices.

With the law of supply and demand in mind, we can immediately understand the value of gold. There has never been a large enough global supply of gold to satisfy everyone's wants, and that inherently makes it valuable.

There is another part of the equation. What causes gold to have a high demand in the first place—other than the fact that it's already valuable? For example, a lot of currencies I listed earlier are valuable because of either (a) something they represent or (b) they are themselves valuable. Situations and circumstances often determine value and influence the law of supply and demand. Cigarettes, for example, are sometimes used as a currency in prisons because they're valuable to the prisoners. In video games and post-apocalyptic movies, bullets are often featured as a form of currency because they are extremely valuable in dangerous scenarios.

What Is Really Housed in Fort Knox?

Gold, of course. Lots of it.

Fort Knox, also known as the United States Bullion Depository, is a military base located in Kentucky. The reserve has about 147.3 million ounces of gold, which is valued at about $187 billion USD as of this writing. (The worth fluctuates as gold prices shift either up or down.)

As hard as it may be to believe, Fort Knox is not considered the largest gold reserve in America. In New York City, located under the subway system, are 508,000 gold bars managed by the Federal Reserve Bank of New York. The New York Federal Reserve does not own the gold or allow private account holders, but rather, safeguards it for account holders such as the US Government, foreign governments, central banks, and various international organizations.

Perhaps in the next James Bond film the villainous Goldfinger will make a comeback and attempt to rob the New York Federal Reserve instead of Fort Knox.

Another aspect necessary for a currency to be effective is that it must be easily carried or transported. This is true of bullets, cigarettes, whale teeth, and obviously coins and paper money—which we'll get to later—but does gold fit into this category? Yes. As mentioned, gold can be smelted into smaller coins or bars and then easily transported by a single person.

There is another reason why gold is considered so valuable as currency: It is extremely difficult or even impossible to reproduce or counterfeit. Safety in a currency relies on the supply remaining stable. If currency is easy to counterfeit, then its value diminishes because anyone can produce it and then people lose trust. As discussed earlier, universal trust in the currency is critical; if it erodes due to counterfeit currency, the entire system is at risk of collapsing.

While there are some minerals and other objects that are similar to gold that could confuse the uninformed, a well-versed businessperson would easily be able to spot forgeries. Today it is quite simple to verify the purity of gold simply by having a scale.

In terms of color, gold and copper are the only metals that are not gray, black, or white—so this alone is an obvious determining factor. Gold is also non-reactive, meaning you cannot extract gold by reacting other elements together.

The only way to find new pure gold is by discovering it in its naturally elemental state. This is incredibly difficult because gold is so rare and hard to find in the wild.

Don't Be a Fool

You may have heard of "fool's gold"—but what is it, exactly? Fool's gold, which messed with prospectors during the California Gold Rush in the late 1840s, is pyrite—a mineral that bears a certain yellowish resemblance to gold. Prospectors discovered some quick tests to distinguish the two, such as hammering the objects: pyrite always breaks into pieces, whereas gold pounds flat.

It is possible to transform some base metals like lead into gold, but this process—known as nuclear transmutation—is so expensive that it costs more to produce the gold than the end product is worth. It is actually much easier to transform gold into lead through nuclear transmutation, which is a foolish exercise in terms of value because the lead is worthless compared to the original gold.

The Gold Standard Isn't So Golden

People often refer to the "gold standard" as meaning "an excellent example of something." For example, one might say a certain type of Jaguar sports car is the "gold standard of luxury vehicles."

When the gold standard is used in the context of currency, it means that the standard monetary system for an entity is backed by gold. For example, if you have $10, that means you have $10 worth of gold. The money in your possession represents an amount of gold that you hypothetically own. In a perfect gold standard economy, you can go to the government and exchange your dollars for an equal amount of gold, since they're always attached to each other and represent the same thing.

The main benefit of the gold standard is that it can stabilize a country's economy and counter inflation, debt, and budget deficits. The negatives far outweigh the positives, however, which is why most countries abandoned the gold standard at some point in the twentieth century.

For one thing, a country's gold reserves are generally fixed or expand slowly. A total of 174,100 tonnes (metric tons) of gold has been mined in human history, and global production in 2011 was 2,700 tonnes. If you have a fixed amount of gold that your money is backed by, then it means you essentially have a fixed money supply. All the money represents is gold; you can inflate the circulation of currency bills or coins all you want, but you can't easily inflate your gold supply.

This is extremely problematic during financial crises and recessions because it hinders the central government's ability to recover. According to Keynesian economic theories (devised by economist John Maynard Keyes), a government would do best by spending money and taking on debt during a recession. The spending should all be poured into public works programs and projects such as infrastructure and parks. Not only does such spending create tons of new jobs, it also gives those people with jobs an income and the ability to spend their money on goods and services, thus increasing the demand for workers in whatever things they choose to spend their money on. It creates a ripple effect and can kick-start a sluggish economy.

If your currency is backed by gold, however, this is incredibly difficult because where does that extra money come from? There's a fixed amount of money because there's a fixed amount of gold.

The second problem is that the price of gold itself is variable. Of course, modern fiat currency valuation fluctuates over time as well. (Just look at the value of the dollar, euro, or pound over the last five years to see evidence of that.) But it's a proven fact that currencies backed by gold fluctuate much more severely; since gold is a resource, the law of supply and demand applies to it. There is infinite demand for money, as everybody has infinite wants. If your money isn't backed by gold and is instead a fiat currency, then its value is backed by the full faith and credit of the government supporting it. The government can artificially alter the supply of money in the economy to whatever levels they think is best. Gold, on the other hand, can vary in quantity.

Take sixteenth and seventeenth century Spain, for example. This country was importing enormous amounts of gold and silver from the New World, which may lead you to believe that it was enormously wealthy. But the law of supply and demand is constant, and the large volume of precious metals flowing into the country created enormous inflation. This had a negative effect on the poorer parts of the population, as goods and services became overpriced.

When this happens it also harms a country's exports, as the expensive goods produced in Spain could not compete with the cheaper goods in foreign countries. The end result was that Spain eventually suffered an economic disaster from the introduction of massive new gold and silver reserves.

The value of gold is not static—and neither is the value of fiat currency—but the value of the former has historically fluctuated much more than of the latter. For these reasons and others, most countries have abandoned the gold standard in favor of fiat-backed currencies.

There is only one country remaining today that is heavily reliant on the gold standard: Lebanon. Nearly 50 percent of its country's economy is backed by gold. And guess what? Lebanon suffers from severe debt as a result, which harms its GDP—especially when the price of gold faces a downward spiral. It seems all that glitters is not truly gold.

HOW MUCH DO YOU KNOW ABOUT GOLD?

1. What actor played the titular character in the James Bond film *Goldfinger*?

2. What is the most expensive gold gadget in the world?

3. From where does the most gold originate?

4. When did the US stop the gold standard?

5. What country has the highest amount of gold reserves?

CHAPTER EIGHT

WHAT IS CREDIT AND WHERE DID IT COME FROM?

Bad debt is debt that makes you poorer. I count the mortgage on my home as bad debt, because I'm the one paying on it. Other forms of bad debt are car payments, credit card balances, or other consumer loans.

—Robert Kiyosaki

Debt and credit are two interconnected things, but their meanings and implications are different. Debt is the amount of money you owe from borrowing it and/or paying interest. Credit, however, is the amount financial institutions, businesses, or individuals will allow you to borrow in order to make purchases, invest, or hire services. Usually these "backers" have something known as a credit limit, which is the maximum they will allow you to borrow on credit. As for debt—well, there really is no limit to that—as many people discover too late and file for bankruptcy and other drastic measures.

You can get credit from anyone or any entity that is willing to lend you the money. The general understanding is that, when you are loaned money, you must pay the amount back within a certain time frame—usually with an additional percentage of money tacked on as a fee for the service of the loan and tying up the funds. This amount is known as *interest*. Depending on the situation and amount, inflated and unregulated interest can be regarded as an illegal practice known as *usury*.

The practice of loaning money has existed at least since the advent of cities thousands of years ago; it likely dates even further back than that. It would have been quite possible for hunter-gatherer tribes with a barter economy system to have lending.

You may be wondering how the above is possible. Let's go back in time and pretend we are hunter-gatherers. I lend you five potatoes today; you pay me back my five potatoes, plus one extra potato in three weeks' time. That's an example of a primitive loan under a barter system, and the concept is pretty comparable when it comes to currency. People with excess money or supplies can benefit by making loans to people who need it on the condition that they will be paid back the full amount and extra at a future time.

The High Price of Defaulting on a Loan

You are probably asking: What happens if I don't pay the person back who loaned me the money or supplies? Well, that depends on a lot of circumstances. If you borrowed money from somebody shady like a loan shark or a gangster, then not paying the money back could potentially endanger your life. This has been true pretty much throughout all history.

In our modern world, as long as you don't borrow from a shady organization or person, your life is not at risk. There are other consequences, however, for failing to pay back a loan...

No Debt Ceiling for These Two Guys

In 2008 Jérôme Kerviel, a trader for Société Générale in France, made illegal trades and forged documents that cost his bank $7.2 billion. Kerviel's salary was only about $66,000 a year, but he was originally convicted and pronounced as owing back almost the full amount of the bank's loss—over $6.2 billion. In 2016 a French court reduced the amount by nearly a fifth, ruling that the bank had greater responsibility for Kerviel's actions as an employee. That is still quite a tidy sum to owe in debt!

As for personal credit: As of 2016, a Santa Clara, CA man named Walter Cavanagh owned nearly 1,500 credit cards granting him a line of credit amounting to $1.7 million. Mr. Cavanagh claims to have a "perfect credit score"—but I wouldn't recommend this as a personal finance strategy to anyone.

For example, if you took out a mortgage—a loan for a house or other residence—and you can't or won't pay that back, then the bank that loaned you the money has the power to evict you from your house and repossess it.

The same is true of a car loan. If you take a loan for a car or other type of vehicle and fail to pay it back, then the organization that provided you with the loan can repossess your car.

Consequences could be even worse than repossession, depending upon whom you took the loan from and under what circumstances. Loan companies can garnish your wages, seize money from your bank accounts, or repossess any item you used as collateral. Failure to pay back loans may harm your credit rating and prevent you from obtaining future loans. You could be taken to court as well.

Centuries of Debt

There is a big difference between a loan payment and debt in terms of duration. Personal debt can last the lifespan of an individual (average 78.4 years in the US vs. 71.5 years worldwide and climbing). Loans, such as mortgages, generally have finite time frames for payment, such as twenty years, thirty years, etc., which can be paid up in one's lifetime.

Debts on a national scale, however, are an entirely different matter; they can literally last for *centuries*. Believe it or not, there are some national debts that are still being paid off that were originally from the seventeenth century! Just imagine debts that predated the founding of the United States. Let's take a look at some of these oddities...

The oldest existing bonds or debts I could find that continue to pay out interest date all the way back to 1624. The Thirty Years' War had just started six years earlier and was still ongoing. Historical figures like Louis XIII and Cardinal Richelieu of France were alive, and the area that is New York City today was first being settled by the Dutch.

And yet, as of this writing in 2017, there is still a bond dating back nearly four centuries to that time. The bond was issued by a seventeenth century water authority (or board) named—brace yourself for this (and I defy you to try to pronounce it)—Hoogheemraadschap Lekdijk Boven dams. This group, which was responsible for maintaining the country's vast system of levies, issued bonds to help pay for the maintenance costs. One such bond dating back to 1648 was written on goatskin. At the time of issuance it was worth 1,000 Dutch Guilders, or a little over $100. The bond was a perpetual bond, meaning that it has no maturity; essentially it can go on forever. Yale University purchased it mostly for the historical value, but in 2015 one of the institution's professors went through the trouble of traveling to the Netherlands to collect twelve years' worth of interest on it, which equaled a whopping $153.

Governments Need Help, Too

Government bailouts are not just a recent occurrence. Back in 1720, a financial panic known as the "South Sea Bubble" occurred. That year, the House of Lords passed the South Sea Bill, granting the South Sea Company a monopoly in trade with South America. The hope was that the results would help subsidize a loan of seven million euros to finance the war against France. Selling of shares ballooned out of control to ten times the original value— and then the bubble burst. The government debt owed from this bailout was outstanding as recently as 2015! The year before the debts were finally fully paid off, there were *11,000 bondholders still collecting interest on the multiple centuries old debts.* Never in its history has Great Britain ever defaulted on any of its debts; this one was no exception, though it did take nearly three centuries to pay it off.

Starting in 1751, Great Britain had another unique form of debt known as a *consol*, a certain British government bond that was redeemable at the option of the government. Consols were perpetual bonds, which means that they had no maturity dates. They could also be treated as equity and not really as debt. Through the Bank of England, the British government took out a number of these types of loans between 1751 and 1923 and only recently paid them all off in 2015.

Britain has also had old bills left over from events and circumstances such as: the Crimean War (1853–1856); the Napoleonic Wars (1803–1815); money loaned to assist Ireland during the Great Famine (1847); and even compensation to slaveholders whose slaves became freed after Britain passed the Slavery Abolition Act of 1833.

The length of loan payback has not been an issue for Great Britain because it has never defaulted on a debt. Britain always pays its debts—even if takes centuries to do it.

Ratings agencies such as Standard & Poor's, Moody's, and Fitch keep tabs on which countries have the best and worst credit ratings. Among the best in recent years with "AAA" ratings are Australia, Canada, and Denmark. The United States, which had been "AAA," was downgraded to "AA+" in 2011 on the heels of the Recession. Among the worst rated are Argentina (with a "CCC"), Pakistan ("B–"), and Egypt ("B–").

These ratings dynamic leads to an unfortunate situation of perpetual poverty for some nations. Countries with high credit scores can continue to borrow money and make good returns on investments, which further increases their wealth and ability to pay back their lenders. Poorer countries, however, find it difficult to borrow money, therefore minimizing their ability to invest in things and lowering their ability to make money on their investments—which harms their ability to pay back potential investors. Depending upon which side of the equation a country is on, this can be a vicious cycle or a really great one. There is no simple solution for balancing out this dynamic.

The Debts That Never End

Right now, there is a woman living in North Carolina named Irene Triplett. Her father, "Uncle" Mose Triplett, was a Civil War veteran who fought on the Confederate side and later defected to the Union. As recently as May 26, 2017, a spokesman for the Department of Veteran Affairs confirmed that Irene Triplett is *still alive and continues to be paid a veteran's pension* inherited from her father.

How is this even possible? Think about this: The Civil War ended over *150 years ago*, but as of this writing (in 2017) the US Government continues to pay a pension for a child of one of the veterans from that war. Do the math: Mose, who was born in 1846, fathered Irene in 1930 at the age of eighty-four with Elda, his (much younger) second wife. Irene, now approaching eighty-seven years of age and very much alive though disabled, receives $73.13 per month from her father's veteran's pension.

The US Department of Veteran Affairs lists the following wars and the number of people that still receiving benefits from them:

- Civil War (1861–1865): one child (Irene Triplett).

- Spanish-American War (1898): forty-six children and forty-two surviving spouses of veterans continue to receive benefits from the war. This is the last war the United States fought in the nineteenth century.

- Mexican Border War (1910–1919): three children and six surviving spouses still receive benefits.

- World War I (1914-1919): 1,590 children and 1,236 surviving spouses still receive benefits.

- World War II (1939-1945): This is the oldest war for which America still has actual surviving veterans. 144,938 veterans continue to receive benefits from the war.

Debt to Pay off War Guilt

When Germany signed the Treaty of Versailles in 1919 following its defeat in WWI, the country agreed to something called the "War Guilt Clause." Germany was deemed responsible for the conflict and had to pay reparations to the victorious powers equal to 132 billion gold marks—or over $400 billion USD, according to current value.

Over the years the Weimar German government defaulted on this debt several times. With the rise of Hitler and the Nazi party in 1933, the reparation payments came to a halt. Starting in the 1950s, however, the West German government began to fulfill these debt obligations once again. West Germany spent decades paying it off, but still hadn't satisfied it by the time the Berlin Wall fell and East and West Germany were reunited. The unified German government continued to pay World War I-era debt until 2010—some ninety-one years after the Treaty of Versailles was signed.

The United States doesn't have war debt in the form of reparations, but it does have a national debt—to the tune of nearly twenty trillion dollars at the time of this writing. About $1.1 trillion of this amount is owed to China, which is a lot of Yuan!

HOW MUCH DO YOU KNOW ABOUT CREDIT?

1. What is the world's largest bank?

2. What is the largest bank in the US?

3. What are the only five countries that have zero debt?

4. In terms of total amount (not vs. GDP), what are the top five countries with the most debt?

5. What is the world's largest credit card company?

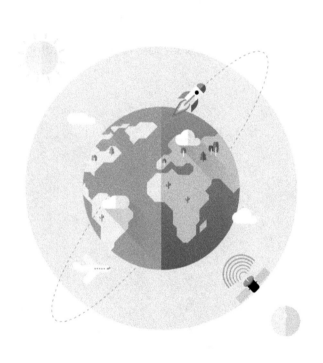

CHAPTER NINE

WHAT IS THE MOST DANGEROUS ROAD IN THE WORLD?

Don't go where the road don't go.

—Ringo Starr

Depending on where you are traveling, driving can be a perfectly safe method of travel—or you may be taking your life into your own hands each time you get behind the wheel. No matter where you live, you have probably experienced at least one or two close calls—if not something worse in the form of an accident or collision—and you've had more than your fill of bad drivers, uttering a few shouts and curses along the way. You may even personally rate drivers in your town, city, state, or country as the "worst." So, what do the statistics and facts have to say about this?

In 2013, there were 1.25 million road traffic deaths across the world. Compare this with airline travel for that same year—statistically, the safest year ever for flying: There were only seventeen airline accidents, totaling only 224 deaths. That's quite a difference, don't you think?

The countries that had the most total driving fatalities that same year were India (207,551) and China (261,367), but this makes sense because they're also the most populated countries in the world. In terms of driving deaths vs. population, the most dangerous country in the world to drive in is Libya, where about 73 out of every 100,000 people in the country die from road accidents. In the United States the number is about 11 people per every 100,000, which means that statistically speaking you're over six times more likely to die in a road accident in Libya than you are in the US

Road traffic accidents kill more people around the world than malaria each year. They are the leading cause of death for people under the age of twenty-nine globally. (They are the fourth for all ages behind heart disease, cancer, and respiratory illness.). Up to fifty million people are also injured every year in road accidents, in addition to the aforementioned 1.25 million who perish each year from road accidents.

Which State in the US Has the Worst Drivers?

If you had to pick a state with the worst drivers, which one comes to mind? New York? New Jersey? Massachusetts? (No offense to anyone from these states....)

It all depends on your perspective, which statistics you are looking at, and the source and year of the data. People may have had experiences with "rude" drivers in a certain state, but that doesn't necessarily mean that's where the most accidents and violations occur.

According to CarInsuranceComparison.com, which in 2016 cited data from the National Highway Transportation Safety Administration (NHTSA), Louisiana and Texas share the top honor. In a different study by SmartAsset in 2017, Florida was cited as the worst due to its high level of traffic violations and uninsured drivers. However, in 2017, EverDrive cited Rhode Island and Connecticut as the two worst. To make this determination even more confusing, the Centers for Disease Control and Prevention (CDC) found in 2015 that West Virginia was the worst state with an accidental death rate at 71.5 deaths per 100,000 residents.

And guess what: If you are going by statistics alone, New York had the *lowest* driving death rate in 2015 at 27.5 per 100,000 residents. In retrospect, you are safer on New York roads than anywhere else in the US—despite all the misperceptions.

Wherever you are driving, this is the main thing to know: Buckle up! It's estimated that half of driving deaths were preventable if passengers had been wearing their seatbelts.

Safer Havens

Okay, all of this talk of car deaths might seem a bit grim and depressing. Let's take a look at the countries that are the *safest*—at least in terms of driving death statistics.

In 2013, the same year we looked at earlier, only one country didn't have any driving fatalities whatsoever:

Monaco. But Monaco is a comparatively small country with a population around only 38,000—so what about a relatively large country?

Not So Safe for a Princess

As we've established, Monaco is a small country known with a good reputation for safe driving. Going back a few years, this may not have always been the case—at least for film legend Grace Kelly, who became a real life princess by marrying the Rainier III, Prince of Monaco. In 1982, Princess Grace accidentally drove her eleven-year-old metallic green Rover 3500 over a cliff in Monaco and died. Her daughter, Stephanie, survived the crash.

The answer for safest country based on a population of 100,000 or more might be Sweden when factoring in years of history. Only 272 driving fatalities were recorded in 2013, which equals just 2.8 driving fatalities per 100,000 people. In 2016, Sweden dropped to number five on the fewest number deaths list with three per 100,000. This is still pretty low, but San Marino had *zero* deaths per 100,000 that same year which is pretty hard to beat!

The Boys That Sang

I know, I promised that this section wouldn't be grim—obviously, I lied.

Sweden may statistically be among the safest places to drive in terms of infrequency of deaths, but one notable English Indie band named Viola Beach ("Boys That Sing") suffered a fatal crash there back in February 2016. All four band members plus Craig Tarry, their manager, perished when their vehicle fell through a gap for boats to pass on the E4 motorway bridge located southwest of Stockholm.

Warning! Dangerous Roads Ahead

Statistically speaking, you are twenty-six times more likely to be killed in a driving accident in Libya than you are in Sweden. But what the most dangerous roads to drive on? Let's take a closer look at the two contenders.

Death Road

La Carretera de los Yungas (a.k.a. "Death Road"), better known as Yungas Road, in Bolivia had a long history of being in the running for the title of "most dangerous road." It is estimated that between 200 and 300 people die per year along this road, which is between 6 percent and 9 percent of all road fatalities in Bolivia for an entire year.

It's easy to see why Yungas Road has such a foul reputation and earned its nickname. In total, two hundred to three hundred people perish along this treacherous road each year.

Yungus Road is a single lane road with few guardrails. The cliffs along Yungas Road stretch up to 1,000 meters (3,281 feet) high. Most of the road is the width of a single vehicle—a mere 3.2 meters (10 feet) wide.

Death road in Bolivia

Driving along Yungas Road is not exactly considered smooth sailing. The road, which extends for 69 kilometers (43 miles) between La Paz and Coroico in Bolivia, consists solely of gravel; none of it is paved.

While the rest of Bolivia drives on the right side of the road, drivers here are required to ride on the left because it is believed they will have a better view of the edge of the road. Descending vehicles never have the right of way on the road; they must move to the outer edge to allow ascending vehicles to pass them.

It gets better—or do I mean *worse*? The most dangerous things about this road are the steep 1,000-meter high cliff on the side and the landslides descending from higher up the mountain. Rain can make the road slippery and wet, and it goes without saying that heavy rain or fog severely hampers visibility. Despite the road's narrow width, it is navigated by trucks, buses, and bikes, as well as automobiles. In 1983, a bus carrying one hundred passengers fell off the road and over the cliff; it was Bolivia's worst road accident ever.

Technically, the danger of Yungus Road has been offset by the construction of a new highway nearby, which redirects traffic. So, the dangers of Death Road are avoidable. Still, I don't think I would ever challenge anyone to a drag race there.

The Deadliest Road Accident Ever

In 1982, a catastrophic road event known as the Salang Tunnel fire occurred during the Soviet invasion of Afghanistan. A lot of details are uncertain about this disaster because the Soviet army didn't record much of what transpired. Suffice to say, this was not your typical road mishap.

The Salang Tunnel, which is located in the Hindu Kush Mountains inside Afghanistan, is nearly three kilometers long. According to Soviet army records, two Soviet military convoys collided inside the tunnel causing a large volume of deaths and a traffic jam. Sixty-four Soviet soldiers and 112 Afghan civilians died from carbon monoxide poisoning inside the tunnel from the idling engines. The death toll in total has been reported anywhere between 176-2,700 people, which is a significant amount of loss either way.

Lost in Alaska

If you happen to be driving through Alaska, you might wish to avoid the James Dalton Highway, another road considered to be among the most dangerous in the world.

Probably the most isolated highway in America, the James Dalton Highway spans 414 miles (666 kilometers) from Fairbanks Alaska to the oil fields near Prudhoe Bay by the Arctic Ocean. There are only three towns along this entire stretch of road with a combined population of just about sixty people: Coldfoot is at mile 175; Wiseman is at mile 188; and then Deadhorse is at the end of the highway at mile 414. If you do trek across this highway, you better remember to fill up as you'll only find three (hopefully open) fuel stops along the entire route—a gas station at mile 56—as well as in Coldfoot and Deadhorse.

The road itself is mostly gravel. Travel by motorcycle or small vehicle is highly discouraged, as it carries significant risks. If anything should go awry, the nearest medical facilities are in Fairbanks and Deadhorse, located on either end of the highway. If you are unfortunate enough to have a medical emergency in the center of the highway, you're 207 miles away from the nearest professional medical help. Anybody embarking on a trip down James Dalton Highway is highly encouraged to bring along survival gear.

James Dalton Highway, Alaska

Not enough to scare you off? How about this: Polar bears have been known to wander near the outskirts of the road. If a polar bear is reported, the road will shut down as wandering bears are an indication that a hunt is in progress. They have been known to attack people along the highway route.

Of course, if you go back a few paragraphs you'll note I did mention that the James Dalton Highway is in Alaska. What do you suppose that means? In addition to everything else I've stated, winter temperatures there can dip down to –80 degrees Fahrenheit (–62 Celsius). I don't think that takes into account wind chill factor.

In summary, if your car breaks down in the middle of the James Dalton Highway this is what you might face: a lengthy span of gravelly road miles away from a gas station and medical help; hungry polar bears on the hunt; and severe tundra-like weather.

Sounds like quite the joy ride, doesn't it?

HOW MUCH DO YOU KNOW ABOUT ROADS?

1. When and where did the joke/riddle "Why did the chicken cross the road?" originate?

2. You've probably heard the expression the "road less traveled"—what is the most traveled road each day in the US?

3. What is the most common street name in the United States?

4. Where did the first auto accident occur?

5. Which city is known for having the most road rage?

CHAPTER TEN

CAN YOU TURN THE EARTH INTO A SANDWICH?

Enjoy every sandwich.

—*Warren Zevon*

Some people like peanut butter and jelly sandwiches. Elvis Presley happened to like his peanut butter sandwich fried with bananas. For many New Yorkers, the ideal sandwich is pastrami on rye with spicy mustard and a sour pickle on the side. If you go to England, the most popular sandwich is cheese (usually cheddar) and onion.

There are millions of mix-and-match sandwich combinations, and what you prepare and eat is all about personal preference. There are few rules when it comes down to the criteria for what makes a "sandwich." In fact, a sandwich may be known under a different term depending upon where you are and the bread being used, as in these examples: a hero (New York City), a sub (New Jersey), a hoagie (Pennsylvania), or a grinder (New England).

The common denominator? A sandwich is two or more slices of bread and some type of filler. Everything else is open to interpretation.

But I've misled you. You've already learned a great deal about sandwiches, but that's not at all the subject of this chapter. We are here to figure out whether it's possible for the planet Earth to be turned into a sandwich (albeit not for consumption).

The Planetary Sandwich Challenge

It would be way too simple for us to just envision two ginormous pieces of sliced bread, place them at opposite ends of the Earth, and call it a sandwich. The challenge is that 71 percent of the Earth's surface is covered in water, which makes finding two opposite ends with solid mass that could serve as "filler" surprisingly difficult.

The Sandwich Origins Controversy

Just for fun, and perhaps because I'm hungry as I write this, let's digress one last time into sandwich lore.

Did the Earl of Sandwich—John Montagu, the 4th Earl of Sandwich—invent his namesake? The answer is *yes...* probably. The *how* is generally what has been disputed. Some historians believe that Montagu specifically asked his cook to create a food item that was easy to hold in his hands while he sat at the gambling table for hours on end. Others insist that it was less of a deliberate "invention"; his servants brought him bread and meat while gambling and others followed suit by saying (okay, I admit I'm paraphrasing): "I'll have what he's having." Still, there are those who assert gambling had nothing to do with the invention at all and the bread/meat concoction was merely something he ate while working at his desk.

One thing we do know: The 4th Earl's sandwich wasn't as elaborate as what you can order today at Subway fast food counters. It was likely toasted bread with a slab of salted beef in the middle.

The *antipode* of any place on Earth is the point on the Earth's surface that is diametrically opposed to it. One antipode would be connected to another by a straight line that runs through the center of the Earth, meaning that if you dug straight down far enough you would eventually reach the opposing point. Such locations are as far away as possible from each other—20,000 kilometers (12,427 miles) across the surface.

Antipode

Two different antipodes are always twelve hours apart. So if it is noon at one point, it means that it's midnight at the other (ignoring daylight savings time, of course). With the exception of the tropics, the longest day at one point corresponds to the shortest day at the other point; the winter solstice coincides with the summer solstice at the other point.

Fifteen percent of the Earth's land is antipodal to other land, while the other 85 percent is opposite ocean on one end or the other. From this 15 percent, these are some of the antipodal cities above which one might be able to place a gigantic piece of bread to create the sandwich:

- Christchurch (New Zealand) and A Coruña (Spain)

- Hamilton (New Zealand) and Cordoba (Spain)

- Hong Kong (China) and La Quiaca (Argentina)

- Junín (Argentina) and Lianyungang (China)

- Madrid (Spain) and Weber (New Zealand)

- Masterton (New Zealand) and Segovia (Spain)

- Nelson (New Zealand) and Mogadouro (Portugal)

- Padang (Indonesia) and Esmeraldas (Ecuador)

- Palembang (Indonesia) and Neiva (Colombia)

- Tauranga (New Zealand) and Jaen (Spain)

- Ulan-Ude (Russia) and Puerto Natales (Chile)

- Wellington (New Zealand) and Alaejos (Spain)

- Whangarei (New Zealand) and Tangier (Morocco)

- Wuhai (China) and Valdivia (Chile)

Is It Possible to Travel by Air Between Antipodes?

There are no non-stop scheduled flights between any two antipodal locations on Earth—or even anything close to that. The longest non-stop scheduled flight was the discontinued Singapore Airlines Flight 21 between Newark New Jersey and Singapore, which spanned 15,343 kilometers (9,534 miles) in about 18.5 hours of flight time; however, this was far from a journey between true antipodes.

There are currently no commercial aircraft capable of traveling between antipodes at full load non-stop. The current record holder is a Boeing 777-200LR (standing for Long Range), which has a maximum range rated at 17,395 kilometers (10,801 miles). Considering that any two antipodes are 20,000 kilometers away, it's still not even close to a single flight.

Hypothetically, the most perfect antipode flight would be from Tangier Ibn Battouta Airport in Morocco to Whangarei Aerodrome, New Zealand. They are about exactly 20,000 kilometers apart from each other and maintain runways that match antipode projections. However, Whangarei's runway is too short to accommodate any current commercial jet airliner.

There are airports that are *close* to being antipodal, but fall just short:

- Taipei, Taiwan and Asuncion, Paraguay: 19,912 kilometers apart

- Santiago, Chile and Xian, China: 19,897 kilometers apart

- Madrid and Auckland: 19,590 kilometers apart

- Buenos Aires and Beijing: 19,260 kilometers apart

- Johannesburg and Honolulu: 19,188 kilometers apart

- New York City and Perth: 18,700 kilometers apart

The largest human inhabited antipodal locations are those of Eastern China/Mongolia and Chile/Argentina. Nearly all of Chile and Argentina are directly opposite Eastern China and a small part of Mongolia and Russia. If you were to dig a hole straight down in Chile or Argentina, odds are that you'd eventually end up in China.

It Possible to Dig to China from the US?

You may have tried this as a kid in your backyard and gave up after creating a crater a couple of feet deep that ruined the lawn and gave you dad fits. But let's suppose you had a super powerful drill (one not yet invented). Could you eventually hit China from somewhere in the United States?

I'm afraid to burst your bubble, but the answer is a resounding *no*. If you dug down anywhere in the United States and continued until you reached the other end, you'd end up in the Indian Ocean.

The only possible way to dig to China (from somewhere outside of China) is to start out in Chile or Argentina. But good luck getting through the Earth's molten core.

Could Any Part of the United States Be Antipodal to a Land Mass?

As we've established, the opposite point on the planet for most places is the ocean. For almost the entirety of the United States, the opposite location of pretty much anywhere would be in the middle of the Indian Ocean and not the misconception of China. The only exceptions:

- Far northern Alaska: antipodal to Antarctica

- Hawaii: antipodal to Botswana and Namibia

- Two small areas in Colorado: antipodal to the volcanic French islands of Ile Amsterdam and Ile Saint Paul

- The town of Rudyard, Montana: antipodal to French Kerguelen Islands in the South Indian Ocean

Rudyard Montana is really the only populated community in the continental United States not antipodal to water. The Kerguelen Islands happen to also be antipodal to some sparsely populated areas in Alberta and Saskatchewan, Canada.

Rudyard, Montana

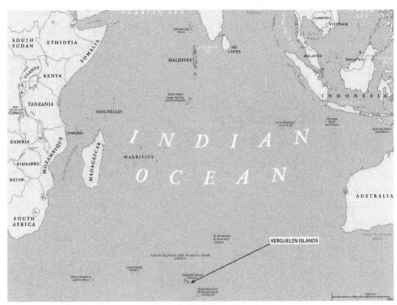

Kerguelen Islands

Since we're on the subject of Canada's antipodes, it's worth mentioning that an area in central Saskatchewan (including the towns of Leask and Shellbrook) is antipodal to uninhabited Australian territory—Heard Island and the McDonald Islands. A large portion of northern Canada and several large islands in the Canadian archipelago are antipodal to Antarctica. Besides that, a vast majority of Canada is antipodal to the southern Indian Ocean.

HOW MUCH DO YOU KNOW ABOUT EARTH?

1. What is the deepest human-made hole in the world?

2. What is the widest human-made hole?

3. What is the deepest natural hole in the world?

4. Was a real sandwich ever eaten in space?

5. Which is the opposite of antipode: (a) posipode (b) podpos (c) there is no such word d) megapode.

CHAPTER ELEVEN

THE LEAST YOU NEED TO KNOW ABOUT EVERY US PRESIDENT

I thought it would be easier.

—Donald Trump, 45th President of the United States

I could write an entire book focusing *RealLifeLore* on the Presidents of the United States. It's a major understatement to say that they are a most fascinating group of individuals—whether history has looked upon their individual reputations and accomplishments as favorable or not.

In order to keep this chapter concise, I've relegated the content to a brief overview of each President, followed by a debunked myth and some lesser-known facts (including pets owned). You can make up your own mind regarding which ones from among the following Presidents you would have voted for, and which ones should be counted as "the best" or "worst."

1. George Washington (1732–1799)

Party: None

Years served: 1789–1797 (two terms)

George Washington

One of America's Founding Fathers, the Commander of the Continental Army, and the first and only non-partisan President. Washington was the only president to be unanimously voted in by the Electoral College—both in 1789 and 1792. He voluntarily stepped down from power after two terms, which established a tradition that would last until 1940 when Franklin Delano Roosevelt served a third term. Washington owned over one hundred slaves, but had them all released in his will after his death.

Myth debunked: Washington never chopped down a cherry tree as a six-year-old. Legend has it that after he allegedly did so he admitted his guilt to his father: "I cannot tell a lie." The story was a fabrication, likely concocted by an early biographer named Mason Locke Weems.

Facts: Washington's nicknames were "Father of His Country" and "American Fabius." Washington was in love with a woman named Sally Fairfax prior to his marriage to

Martha. Washington had parrots, dogs, horses, and even a donkey. He was especially fond of hunting and dogs and may have had as many as fifty total over his life span. One of his beloved dogs was a Dalmatian named Madame Moose.

2. John Adams (1735–1826)

Party: Federalist
Years *served:* 1797–1801 (one term)

John Adams was a Founding Father who served as America's first Vice President under George Washington before he was elected President. Adams was the father of John Quincy Adams, the sixth President of the United States, and cousin of statesman Sam Adams. He never owned slaves and was the first President to reside in the actual White House. Adams assisted Thomas Jefferson in the writing of the *Declaration of Independence* and, in fact, both died on the same day—which also happened to be the 50th anniversary of the document's adoption.

Myth debunked: John Adams is a widely celebrated Founding Father in Washington, D.C.: *not!* Despite his myriad accomplishments, Adams is one of the few significant leaders from the Colonial Era without a proper memorial. An Adams Memorial was authorized in 2001 and renewed in 2014—yet as of this date construction has not begun.

Facts: In 1770 Adams defended nine British soldiers charged with the deaths of five colonists in the Boston massacre. Adams had both horses and dogs. One of his canines was named Satan.

3. Thomas Jefferson (1743–1826)

Party: Democratic–Republican
Years served: 1801–1809 (two terms)

Thomas Jefferson

Jefferson was a Founding Father and the main author of the Declaration of Independence, which was adopted on July 4, 1776. He served as Vice President under John Adams. Jefferson organized the Louisiana Purchase from Napoleon, which almost doubled the size of the country. He banned new slaves from being imported into the United States—but was a plantation owner himself with several hundred slaves. He is believed to have had a romantic relationship with Sally Hemings, one of his slaves.

Myth debunked: Thomas Jefferson never freed Sally Hemings, whom many historians believe was the mother of one or more of Jefferson's children.

Fact: : Jefferson did free Sally Hemings' children (Beverly and Harriet during his lifetime; Madison and Eston in his will.) Among Jefferson's pets: a mockingbird; two bear cubs; dogs; and horse named Caractacus (named after a first century British tribal leader).

4. James Madison (1751–1836)

Party: Democratic-Republican
Terms: 1809–1817 (two terms)

James Madison was a Founding Father who also became known as both the "Father of the Bill of Rights" and "Father of the Constitution," due to his advocacy for the documents (although Jefferson mainly penned most of the latter). Madison resided over the War of 1812 with the United Kingdom in which the Americans attempted to conquer Canada but failed. Madison owned several hundred slaves during his lifetime.

Myth debunked: Madison's wife, Dolley, personally had nothing to do with the Dolly Madison Bakery or the ice cream products. Her likeness was used in connection with branding, but the spelling of her name was changed to *Dolly* without the *e*.

Dolly Madison on 1980's US postage stamp

Fact: Madison was our shortest President at 5'4." Dolley Madison, known for her charm, is largely regarded as the woman who defined the role of "First Lady." Predictably, James Madison's pet parrot was named Polly.

5. James Monroe (1817–1825)
Party: Democratic-Republican
Terms: 1817–1825 (two terms)

Monroe was the last President who was a Founding Father. He bought Florida from Spain, occupied the Oregon territory with Britain, and established the 49th parallel with British Canada—a border that still exists today. He supported the founding of colonies in Africa for freed American slaves, which would eventually form the nation of Liberia—whose capital, Monrovia, is named in his honor. Monroe established the Monroe Doctrine, which stated that the United States would not accept the establishment of new colonies by European powers in the Western Hemisphere.

Myth debunked: Some people believe that Monroe's election to a second term was not unanimous because one elector didn't want anyone other than George Washington to have been elected unanimously. This was not the case: William Plumer cast his electoral ballot for John Quincy Adams because he thought he would be a superior President.

Facts: Monroe served with distinction and fought several battles in the Revolutionary War, including under George Washington. He had a shrapnel injury in his shoulder that remained for his entire life. Monroe had two dogs. And what was his death date? You guessed it: July 4, just like John Adams and Thomas Jefferson (though not the same year).

6. John Quincy Adams (1767–1849)
Party: Democratic-Republican
Term: 1825–1829 (one term)

John Quincy Adams was the son of the second US President, John Adams. Not too much happened during his presidency, except that he paid off most of the national debt. Adams lost his re-election bid to Andrew Jackson, after which he served seventeen years as US Representative for the state of Massachusetts. Adams was a staunch opponent of slavery.

Myth debunked: Adams' nickname may have been "Old Man Eloquent," but by most accounts (including himself, in his own diary) he was a terrible conversationalist.

Facts: Adams was the first President to be photographed. He had a pet alligator in the White House, as well as silkworms.

7. Andrew Jackson (1767-1845)
Party: Democrat
Terms: 1829-1837 (two terms)

Andrew Jackson

Jackson was founder of the modern Democrat party. During his administration, South Carolina threatened to secede; Jackson threatened military action and it stopped. He was responsible for the Trail of Tears after signing the Itribes to Oklahoma. Jackson was the only president to preside while the national debt was fully paid off.

Myth debunked: Jackson goes against the myth that all Presidents have been "well educated." He only had a modicum of classroom education and was largely self-educated.

Facts: Jackson is the face of the $20 bill until 2020 when he will be replaced by Harriet Tubman. He participated in at least thirteen duels during his lifetime; in one winning encounter, he received a chest wound that remained with him for the rest of his life. Jackson was the first President to have been the victim of an assassination attempt; the assassin's pistols backfired and Jackson nearly beat the assassin to death with his cane before the secret service pulled him away. He experienced a scandal because his wife was already legally married to someone else when he married her. Jackson had horses, fighting cocks, and a parrot named Polly who was taught to swear (which he did at the President's own funeral).

8. Martin Van Buren (1782–1862)
Party: Democrat
Term: 1837–1841 (one term)

Van Buren was also one of the early founders of the Democratic party. He served as a US Senator and as both Vice President and Secretary of State under Andrew Jackson. Van Buren refused to admit Texas into the Union because of the balance of power between free and slave states. Not much else really happened during his presidency.

Myth debunked: It has been speculated by some people that Van Buren's father was noted womanizer Aaron Burr (the politician who killed Alexander Hamilton in a duel), but there is no concrete evidence to support this.

Facts: Van Buren was the first President born after the founding of America. His nickname was "Old Kinderhook." (Some historians/linguists speculate this led to the expression "OK"). He had two tiger cubs, but Congress coerced him into donating them to a zoo.

9. William Henry Harrison (1773-1841)

Party: Whig

Term: March 4, 1841-April 4, 1841 (died on his thirty-second day in office)

Harrison was the first Whig candidate elected President and the last who was born a British subject. What the heck was a Whig, you are afraid to ask? A Whig was an anti-Democratic party that supported economic expansion and decreased power of the presidency vs. that of legislation. Harrison's Presidential term is notable for being the shortest in history; he served only thirty-two days at office before he died. He delivered the longest inaugural address in history, speaking for two hours wearing just a shirt and no coat or gloves in the dead of winter.

Myth debunked: Did Harrison die from pneumonia as a result of his inaugural speech? Maybe...but now many medical expertise theories that he died from typhoid (enteric fever).

Facts: Harrison was the oldest President up until his time at at sixty-eight. Harrison's nickname was "Old Tip." What could he accomplish in thirty-two days as President? Not much—and he didn't. Harrison had a cow named Sukey and a goat.

10. John Tyler (1790-1862)

Party: Whig (for five months, no party rest of office)

Term: 1841-1845 (one term)

Tyler, who was the first Vice President to succeed to the Presidency without being elected, does not fare well in ratings of Presidents. He annexed the Republic of Texas into the Union during his last days in office. He shocked his own Whig party by deciding that most of the Whig platform was unconstitutional. He was expelled from the party only five months after taking office and thus became known as the man without a party. Tyler was the first President whose veto was overridden by Congress.

Myth debunked: Some people may believe that John Tyler was impeached. He wasn't, though he was known for being the first President for which it was proposed. He's no relation to Aerosmith's singer Steven Tyler. (Wait, did anyone really think that?)

Facts: Tyler's unfavorable nickname was "His Accidency." He considered himself something of a political Robin Hood and even named his Virginia Plantation Sherwood Forest. Later in life, he ran for a Confederate office—which made him even less popular. Tyler had a dog, a canary, and a horse.

11. James K. Polk (1795-1849)
Party: Democrat
Term: 1845-1849 (one term)

Before he was President, Polk was the 13th Speaker of the House of Representatives and Governor of Tennessee. He ran on a campaign to complete the annexation of Texas and the promise he would only serve one term. When Mexico rejected the US Annexation of Texas, Polk led the nation into the Mexican-American War, which lasted from 1846 to 1848. The United States occupied a large part of Mexico and even captured Mexico City, which ended the war. Mexico gave up nearly half of its territory to the US after the war was over, including the modern states of California, Arizona, Nevada, Utah, New Mexico, and parts of Wyoming and Colorado. Polk also threatened war with the United Kingdom over the status of the Oregon territory, but Great Britain backed down and agreed to sell the territory to the US. Polk kept his campaign promise and stepped down after this first term in office. He died only months later from cholera.

Myth debunked: Polk is hardly spoken about these days not because he was a bad President; in fact, he's known for several successes (e.g., expanding US territory) and largely kept to his word. The main reason he's not discussed much is because he *did* keep to his word and didn't run for a second term.

Facts: Polk was known for a strange hairstyle that was part mullet and part pre-hippie, running in a slight curve down the back of his neck. Polk had horses.

James K. Polk

12. Zachary Taylor (1784–1850)
Party: Whig
Term: 1849–1850 (died seventeen months into office)

Taylor was noted for being a hero of the Indian wars and as a successful general during the Mexican-American War. He wasn't particularly interested in politics, and had very vague political beliefs. He had an unclear platform and, despite owning 200 slaves in his lifetime, didn't push for the expansion of slavery.

Myth debunked: Taylor's death in 1850 while in office remains unproven. At a ceremony for the Washington Monument, he ate a huge bowl of cherries and drank an entire pitcher of milk. Doctors at the time thought this strange mixture took his life, but today it is more commonly believed that cholera did him in.

Facts: One of Taylor's ancestors was Elder William Brewster, a pilgrim aboard the Mayflower. He was also second cousin to President James Madison. Taylor's nickname was "Old Rough and Ready" and he had a horse named Old Whitey.

13. Millard Fillmore (1800-1874)
Party: Whig
Term: 1850-1853 (one term)

Fillmore succeeded to the Presidency after Zachary Taylor died, subsequent to having served as Vice President under him. He was the last Whig President and the last to not be affiliated with either the Democrat or Republican parties. He is the only Whig President who did not die in office or get expelled from the party. He signed the Fugitive Slave Act, which required that free northerners return escaped slaves to their southern masters.

Myth debunked: Journalist/satirist H.L. Mencken is presumed to have created the myth that Fillmore installed the first bathroom in the White House.

Facts: Fillmore is rated at the bottom of the barrel among US Presidents—in no small part due to his position on slavery. There was no Vice President under Fillmore during his term. Fillmore had ponies named Mason and Dixon.

14. Franklin Pierce (1804-1869)
Party: Democrat
Term: 1853-1857 (one term)

Pierce was a US Senator for New Hampshire prior to becoming President. Pierce was strongly against abolition during his time as a legislator. He witnessed his son's death in a train accident shortly before his inauguration. Pierce supported slavery and worked to fight the abolitionist movement. He signed the Gadsden Purchase, which created the modern borders of Arizona and New Mexico. He attempted to annex Cuba from Spain and turn it into a slave state, but the effort failed. He signed the Kansas-Nebraska Act, which allowed Kansas to join the Union and vote on becoming a slave or free state. This led to thousands on both sides flooding to Kansas to vote on the issue and produced riots and violence. Pierce became the only President not to be re-nominated by his party for a second term in office.

Myth debunked: Some rumors have it that President Pierce killed an old woman either while on horseback or with a carriage. There is no substantiation for this assertion.

Facts: Despite the fact that Pierce was known during his time to be charming and handsome, Pierce's (rather dubious) legacy as President has faded into oblivion and he is rated among the worst. Nicknamed "Young Hickory of the Granite Hills," Pierce had both dogs and birds.

15. James Buchanan (1791-1869)
Party: Democrat
Term: 1857-1861 (one term)

Though it may be hard to believe, Buchanan is the only President to hail from the state of Pennsylvania. Prior to his Presidency, Buchanan was the 17th United States Secretary of State. He also served in the United States Senate and the United States House of Representatives.

He served as President immediately prior to the Civil War, and his indecisiveness on slavery alienated both sides. He promised to serve only one term and he did, voluntarily stepping aside to allow his Vice President to run for office in 1860. When Republican Abraham Lincoln won the election with the promise of stopping the expansion of slavery any further West, seven Southern states seceded during the final days of Buchanan's administration. He thought that secession was illegal, but going to war to stop secession was also illegal. So he did nothing and left office pretty much disgraced.

Myth debunked: Was Buchanan our only homosexual President? Not that there is anything wrong with it (although there certainly *would* have been by 1850's American social mores), but there is no evidence of this assertion. Some people point to facts such as, that he was a lifelong bachelor (albeit engaged once) and roomed with William Rufus King of Alabama for years. Some politicians referred to the two men as "The Siamese Twins" and others taunted King with names like "Miss Nancy," "Aunt Fancy," and "Mrs. Buchanan."

Facts: Buchanan, the last President born in the eighteenth century, was the only president to remain a lifelong bachelor. He had dogs and an eagle.

16. Abraham Lincoln (1809-1865)
Party: Republican
Term: 1861-1865 (assassinated in office)

Abraham Lincoln

What is there to say about President Lincoln that we don't already know? He was a lawyer, but you may be unaware that he didn't have a legal degree. He served in the House of Representatives for many years, during which time he was primarily a member of the Whig party. Lincoln won the Presidential election in 1860, but before he even assumed office in March 1861, seven southern states had already seceded and created the Confederacy. In April, just one month after he assumed office, the Confederacy attacked Fort Sumter—the start of the Civil War. Lincoln served as President during the entire war, which saw the deaths of 785,000 to one million people—more deaths than America suffered in both World Wars combined. (A war fought on the same scale today with a proportionate number of deaths would be around nine million people dead.) Lincoln established the Emancipation Proclamation, delivered the famous Gettysburg Address, and pushed the

13th amendment through Congress, which permanently outlawed slavery in the US He won re-election, but was assassinated only five days after the end of the Civil War.

Myth debunked: Rumors occasionally crop up that Lincoln was homosexual (he was married with children), but this is unsubstantiated. (Larry Kramer, a gay rights activist, speculated on this.) Lincoln was also by no means a "simple country lawyer"; he was quite shrewd and made a good living at practicing law.

Facts: Lincoln, the first President to have been assassinated (by John Wilkes Booth), is often regarded as our greatest President for having ended slavery and done what was necessary to end the Civil War. Lincoln was our tallest President at 6'4" and something of a wrestler. He was a devout reader of the Bible, but didn't belong to a specific church. He didn't smoke or drink. He had cats, dogs, goats (Nanny and Nanko), a turkey, and a rabbit. Lincoln once quipped that one of his cats, Dixie, was smarter than his whole cabinet.

17. Andrew Johnson (1808-1875)
Party: Republican
Term: 1865-1869 (continued Lincoln's term)

Johnson was the Vice President under Lincoln and succeeded him after his assassination in 1865. He wanted to quickly bring back the southern states into the Union and wasn't interested in protecting former slaves. He opposed the 14th Amendment, which gave citizenship to former slaves, and allowed the Southern states to discriminate against newly freed black slaves. He was the first President to be impeached with only one naysayer in the Senate. He retired from the Presidency after his first term and declined to run for office.

Myth debunked: Of all the negative things said about Johnson, the one that probably isn't true is that he once "pardoned a vampire." An article in the November 4, 1892 *Brooklyn Daily Eagle* apparently started this bizarre story, in which Johnson is said to have pardoned a man in 1867 who had killed two sailors and drank their blood.

Facts: Johnson frequently heads the list of "worst Presidents." Why was he so awful and impeached? He broke the Tenure of Office Act, which had been created to ensure the President wouldn't fire Senate-confirmed officials without their approval. While Congress was out of session, he fired Secretary of War Edward Stanton, replacing him with Ulysses Grant. Well, this didn't sit well with Stanton (or anyone else) who refused to step down. Johnson tried again, this time inserting Adjutant-General Lorenzo Thomas. The move was viewed as the last straw and impeachment proceedings began. Interestingly, the Tenure of Office Act was later repealed. On another important subject: Johnson didn't have any official pets...but he reportedly fed mice in his bedroom.

18. Ulysses S. Grant (1822-1885)
Party: Republican
Term: 1869-1877 (two terms)

Grant was the commanding Union general during the Civil War. He had some major accomplishments as President, including the enforcement of civil rights and voting rights in the South using the US Army, as well as, his prosecution of the KKK. On the other hand, he went to war with Native Americans on the frontier (which included the Battle of Little Bighorn); attempted to annex the Dominican Republic into the US but failed; and is largely thought to have been corrupt.

Myth debunked: To this day, some people hold onto the fact that the "S" stood for something (such as Simpson). It didn't stand for anything at all. His full name was Hiram Ulysses Grant, so his middle name was actually *Ulysses*.

Facts: Grant, a graduate of West Point, was an alcoholic. Grant was supposed to be at Ford Theater when Lincoln was assassinated but went with other plans. Grant had several dogs, horses, and ponies.

19. Rutherford B. Hayes (1822-1893)
Party: Republican
Term: 1877-1881 (one term)

Hayes was an attorney and Governor of Ohio prior to becoming President. He won the election in one of the most contentious ever, losing the popular vote but narrowly winning in the Electoral College. He oversaw the end of the Reconstruction. Hayes ended US Military occupation in the South. He pledged not to run for re-election and retired from the presidency after his first term.

Myth debunked: Hayes was not actually sworn in during the inauguration on March 5, 1877. The swearing in occurred two days prior on March 3 in a private ceremony. Some believe the shift happened because Hayes was threatened following a hotly contested election.

Facts: Hayes fought in the Civil War and received numerous injuries; he was once hurt so badly he was reported to have been killed. Hayes was the opposite of his predecessor, alcoholic President Grant, and became a teetotaler, banning alcohol at the White House. For this reason, he earned the nickname "Old Granny" and his wife was dubbed "Lemonade Lucy." Hayes started many Presidential "firsts," including the traditional "Easter Eggs Roll." He owned several dogs and cats. One of his cats was a gift from the King of Siam named Miss Pussy.

20. James A. Garfield (1831-1881)

Party: Republican

Term: March 1881-September 1881 (assassinated in office)

James A. Garfield was a Union general who served nine terms in the House of Representatives prior to becoming President. He served only six months as President before he was assassinated. He thus became the second President whose life was taken while in office.

Myth debunked: Garfield was shot twice at a train station by a drifter named Charles Guiteau. Garfield survived for 80 days until he actually died. But should the bullets have claimed his life? In all probability, the cause of the President's death was an infection due to medical negligence (the doctor's hands were not sterile, for example) and a box spring that interfered with a metal detector device intended to find the second bullet in his body.

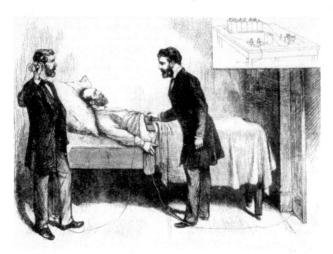

James A. Garfield examined by Alexander Graham Bell seeking to locate assassin's bullet with electrical detector, 1881

Facts: 1881 marked the only year in US history the country had *three* Presidents: Hayes, Garfield, and Chester A. Arthur. Garfield was the only President who was a preacher (i.e., a minister of the Christian Church). Garfield had a horse as well as a dog, Veto.

21. Chester A. Arthur (1829-1886)
Party: Republican
Term: 1881-1885 (assumed presidency after Garfield's death)

Chester A. Arthur was an attorney before he became Vice President under Garfield. He succeeded to the office after Garfield's assassination. Arthur installed the civil service system (government jobs assigned by merit) and prosecuted post office fraud.

Myth debunked: : Barack Obama was not the first President falsely charged with "Birther" claims of not having been born in the US. Some claimed Chester Arthur was born in Canada, while others said Ireland. The truth is that he was born in Vermont.

Facts: Arthur had many nicknames, including "Prince Arthur," "the Dude President," and "Walrus." He suffered the loss of a son at three years of age. His wife died of pneumonia one year before he became President. He never had a Vice President during his Presidency. He had a rabbit and horses.

22. Grover Cleveland (1837-1909)
Party: Democrat
Term: 1885-1889 (one term)

Cleveland was a teacher, an attorney, a sheriff (Erie County), a mayor (Buffalo), and a governor (New York) prior to becoming President. He was the only president who ever served nonconsecutive terms. He won three popular votes for President: in 1884, 1888 (lost by Electoral College), and 1892. He became the first Democrat to become President since the Civil War. Cleveland reversed orders by President Arthur and returned lands to Native Americans.

Grover Cleveland

Myth debunked: Cleveland's real name was Stephen, not Grover.

Facts: Cleveland was a direct descendant of Moses Cleveland, who founded Ohio. As a sheriff, he personally hanged two convicted murderers to save money for an executioner. Cleveland was a pretty large guy who weighed 250 pounds. In 1885 he became the only President to have married in the White House (in the blue room, to Frances Folsom). He confessed to the possibility that he might have fathered an illegitimate child. Cleveland owned dogs and mockingbirds. For more information, see President number 24.

23. Benjamin Harrison (1833–1901)
Party: Republican
Term: 1889–1893 (one term)

Benjamin Harrison was the grandson of deceased President William Henry Harrison. He raised tariffs and increased federal spending, which decreased his popularity and led him to lose re-election.

Myth debunked: Some people hold onto the belief that Harrison tried to create East and West Dakota but, in fact, he wrote Proclamation 292 admitting North Dakota into the Union, thereby dividing North and South Dakota.

Facts: Harrison was the first President to have had electricity in the White House. He was known for a harsh personality and was dubbed "the Human Iceberg." After his wife passed away, Harrison married her niece who was thirty years his junior. He was a born-again Christian and a relative of televangelist Pat Robertson. He had a goat named Whiskers, two opossums (Mr. Reciprocity and Mr. Protection), and a Collie named Dash.

24. Grover Cleveland (1837–1909)
Party: Democrat
Term: 1893–1897 (one term)

Grover Cleveland won the Presidency a second term after Benjamin Harrison. He accomplished a great deal to establish government infrastructure, including creation of the Interstate Commerce Commission and initiating improvements on the Navy.

Myth debunked: Cleveland was not related to the Hall of Fame Major League pitcher who had a similar name, Grover Cleveland Alexander.

Facts: In 1893, Cleveland had a tumor on the roof of his mouth that required surgery. The procedure was performed in secret aboard a yacht to prevent panic. Not even his Vice President, Adlai Stevenson, was aware of the surgery— which, fortunately, ended up being a success. For more information, see President number 22.

25. William McKinley (1843–1901)
Party: Republican
Term: 1897–1901 (assassinated six months into second term)

William McKinley was the last President to have served in the Civil War. He led the U.S. into the Spanish–American war, which the US won. The US annexed Puerto Rico, Guam, and the Philippines in the aftermath of the war. The US Military occupied Cuba, but promised the country independence. He also oversaw the annexation of Hawaii into the US. He won re-election for a second term, but was assassinated by a Polish–American anarchist named Leon

Czolgosz only six months into his second term. He became the third president to be assassinated while in office.

Myth debunked: What was the cause of McKinley's death? It was originally believed that the bullet wound penetrated various vital organs, which led to his death. More likely, he suffered an infection from the wound and died of pancreatic necrosis.

Facts: Mount McKinley in Alaska, which was originally named after him by a prospector named William Dickey, is now known as Denali (though some current politicians have expressed an interest in reverting it back to Mount McKinley.) McKinley had a parrot, kittens, and roosters.

26. Theodore Roosevelt (1858-1919)
Party: Republican
Term: 1901-1909 (two terms; succeeded McKinley after his assassination)

Theodore Roosevelt

Theodore "Teddy" Roosevelt was a larger-than-life figure: a soldier, a naturalist, an explorer, and an author, in addition to becoming President. He remains the youngest person to ever become the President, as he was forty-two-years-old at the time of his inauguration. He established many national parks, started construction of the Panama Canal, and greatly expanded the US Navy. He groomed William Taft as his successor, but changed his mind when he grew frustrated with how Taft was handling things and ran for a third term in 1912. He lost the Republican nomination and started the Bull Moose Party to run on. He won 27 percent of the vote—more than the Republicans had—but less than the Democrats. Roosevelt became the first US President to be awarded the Nobel Peace Prize for mediating an end to the Russo-Japanese War.

Myth debunked: Although Roosevelt campaigned on the "Bull Moose Party" ticket" for a third term, he never actually rode a moose—as had been depicted in cartoons and doctored photographs.

Facts: While campaigning independently for his third term, a crazed man shot him in the chest while he was delivering a speech. Roosevelt continued to give his speech for ninety minutes after being wounded; blood seeped through his shirt and he only went to the hospital after he finished the last word. Roosevelt held a black belt in jiu-jitsu and was a champion boxer. He was the first President to drive a car and fly aboard a plane. He had a zoo full of pets: guinea pigs, ponies, dogs, cats, snakes, a hyena, a hen, a one-legged rooster, a pig, a rabbit, a badger, a lizard, a bear, a rat, a badger, a wild cat, a coyote, a zebra, and a barn owl.

27. William Howard Taft (1857-1930)

Party: Republican
Term: 1909-1913 (one term)

William Taft was the successor to Roosevelt. After he lost re-election in 1912 because of Roosevelt splitting the Republican vote, he became the Chief Justice of the United

States—the only person to ever hold both offices during his lifetime. He preferred this role to being President.

Myth debunked: Due to his immense size, rumors spread that he was once "stuck" in a bathtub and had to be pried out. This couldn't be true, as the White House bathtub was enormous (even for someone of his girth).

Facts: Taft, nicknamed "Big Bill" and "Big Lub," was America's heaviest President, weighing 340 pounds at one point during his presidency. He was the first President to throw out the first pitch at a baseball game. He was also the first president buried in Arlington Cemetery. Taft had a dog named Caruso and two cows, Mooly Wooly and Pauline Wayne.

28. Woodrow Wilson (1856-1924)
Party: Democrat
Terms: 1913-1921 (two terms)

Woodrow Wilson was the first Southerner to be elected President since Zachary Taylor in 1848. Wilson was a historian, political scientist, and the Governor of New Jersey prior to becoming President. He maintained a policy of US neutrality with the outbreak of WWI. In 1916 he won re-election to a second term, becoming the first Democrat since Andrew Jackson to serve two consecutive terms. He asked Congress to declare war on Germany in April 1917 after the Zimmerman telegraph (Germany's potential alliance with Mexico) and Germany's unrestricted submarine warfare. He endorsed the 19th Amendment which, in 1920, gave women the right to vote in the US for the first time. He promoted the League of Nations, which was ultimately voted down by the US Senate. He became the second sitting US President to be awarded the Nobel Peace Prize for his efforts. Prohibition was also passed during his second term in 1919 and went into effect in 1920.

Myth debunked: Wilson's political enemies created the falsehood that Wilson had an affair with silent film star Florence La Badie and then had her murdered. Not true: She died in a car accident.

Facts: Wilson is the only President buried in Washington, DC. He had dogs, a ram (Old Ike), a cat (Puffins), songbirds, and sheep.

29. Warren G. Harding (1865–1923)

Party: Republican

Term: 1921–1923 (one term, died while in office)

Warren G. Harding

Warren G. Harding, a US Senator prior to becoming President, is often rated among the worst Presidents in US history due to his myriad scandals. He was implicated in numerous corruption acts and extramarital affairs, which didn't come to light until after his death from a heart attack while in office. (We'll go with this over cerebral hemorrhage, which some sources state.) His reputation suffered mostly from exposure in the Teapot Dome scandal when his Secretary of the Interior, Albert Bacon Fall, was caught giving leases as bribes to two of his friends in Naval Reserves in Wyoming.

Myth debunked: Some unsubstantiated rumors have it that Harding was murdered by his jealous wife. She didn't—but, based on his myriad infidelities, who would have blamed her if she had done the deed?

Facts: Harding had sexual relations with a woman named Nan Britton and fathered her child. He and Nan regularly had sex in a White House closet. He also had an affair with the wife of a friend, James Phillips. Harding was as famous for his crassness as his libido, referring to one mistress's genitalia as "Mrs. Pouterson" and to his own penis as "Jerry." He had the largest feet of any President (size 14). Harding was an ardent poker player and is believed to have lost the White House China in a card game. Despite his massive unpopularity, Harding is buried in a lavish grave in Marion, OH. Harding had dogs and a canary.

30. Calvin Coolidge (1872–1933)
Party: Republican
Terms: 1923–1929 (two terms, succeeded Harding after his death)

Calvin Coolidge was a lawyer and the Governor of Massachusetts prior to serving as Vice President under Warren G. Harding and then succeeding him after his death. He was the first President born after the Civil War had ended. His greatest accomplishments were lowering the US debt, reducing taxes, and shrinking the budget.

Myth debunked: Over the years, some Republicans (including President Ronald Reagan) have held Coolidge in high regard as a model for the party (small government, low taxes). While there is some truth to this, the reasons behind Coolidge's philosophy were more attributable to the times (the 1920's) than his permanent ideology for the party.

There is also the issue that the Depression occurred right after he left office and Hoover became President: Should *all* of the blame go to Hoover for what he inherited?

Facts: Coolidge, nicknamed "Silent Cal," was reserved but something of a prankster. He would buzz the Secret Service and then hide, making them think he was taken hostage. Coolidge had a wild array of pets, including a black bear, several dogs, two raccoons (Rebecca and Horace), a donkey (Ebeneezer), canaries, a goose (Enoch), a bobcat (Smoky), a housecat (Tiger), two lion cubs (Tax Reduction and Budget Bureau), a pygmy hippopotamus (Billy), a wallaby, and a duiker (antelope).

31. Herbert Hoover (1874–1964)
Party: Republican
Term: 1929–1933 (one term)

Herbert Hoover

Herbert Hoover was Secretary of Commerce prior to becoming President at the beginning of the Great Depression in the United States. The Wall Street crash of 1929 happened eight months into his term. Hoover was unable to reverse the damage of the Depression. His popularity declined even more due to his increasingly unpopular prohibition policies. As a result, he suffered an overwhelming defeat to Roosevelt in the 1932 election. Hoover is known for having started construction on the Hoover Dam.

Myth debunked: Right or wrong, Hoover usually gets lumped at the bottom of the Presidential barrel as among the worst. To be fair, he didn't cause the Depression—and he tried several methods of resolving it that were later expanded upon by his successor, Franklin Delano Roosevelt. He also made a number of decisions that backfired (e.g., an ill-conceived tariff that made the Depression even worse). But his greatest failing was his communication style; he inadvertently came across as cold and uncaring to his poverty-stricken citizens.

Facts: Hoover lost his father at six and became an orphan at nine. He was a self-made millionaire who donated all of the money he made from the Presidency to charity. Hoovervilles were the thousands of shanty towns named in Hoover's honor during the Depression. On the plus side, Hoover was known all over the world as a humanitarian and was nominated five times for the Nobel Peace Prize. (He never won.) He had a number of dogs, including a Belgian Shepherd named King Tut. He also had two alligators.

32. Franklin D. Roosevelt (1882-1945)
Party: Democrat
Terms: 1933-1945 (four terms, died in his fourth term)

Franklin Delano Roosevelt (FDR) was Governor of New York prior to winning an unprecedented four US Presidential elections. FDR is the only President to have ever served more than two terms. He instituted the New Deal, which greatly helped reverse the Great Depression. The repeal of Prohibition in 1933 contributed to his popularity. FDR passed the first federal minimum wage and signed the Social Security Act. He had a policy of neutrality during WWII, although he sent weapons to Britain and China. The day after Japan bombed Pearl Harbor on December 7, 1941, he rallied Congress to declare war on Japan. Meanwhile, Nazi Germany and Italy both declared war on the US. He mobilized the US economy to help with the war effort. During the war years, he ordered the internment of over 100,000 Japanese American civilians. He also oversaw the development of the world's first nuclear bomb. The unemployment rate went down from 25% when he took office to only 2 percent during the war. He served three full terms and was reelected to a fourth, but he died from illness three months into this term before the war was over.

Franklin D. Roosevelt

Myth debunked: Modern scientists may never know for sure—but they are currently rebuking the idea that FDR suffered from polio. Instead, they believe the President's paralysis was likely caused by Guillain-Barre Syndrome (GBS), an autoimmune disorder in which the immune system attacks the nervous system.

Facts: FDR fared poorly at Columbia Law School; although he passed the Bar, he never received his degree. The 22nd

Amendment now ensures that no one can serve more than two terms as President. FDR was an avid stamp collector. He was distantly related to his wife, Eleanor Roosevelt, who also happened to be the niece of another of FDR's distant relatives, President Theodore Roosevelt. FDR's twenty-eighty radio speeches were known as "Fireside Chats" and were an intimate way for the President to communicate with the American people. He was known by a number of nicknames, most of which were positive: "That Man in the White House," "Sphinx," and "Houdini in the White House." Roosevelt had many dogs, including a Great Dane he called President.

33. Harry Truman (1884-1972)

Party: Democrat
Terms: 1945-1953 (two terms, succeeded Roosevelt after he died)

Harry Truman fought in France during WWI, owned a haberdashery, and became a Senator prior to becoming Vice President under FDR. He succeeded FDR when he died during his fourth term. He was President during the final months of WWII and approved the plans to drop atomic bombs on Hiroshima and Nagasaki. He was elected in his own right in 1948 and was in office at the beginning of the Cold War with the Soviet Union. He helped found the United Nations in 1945, issued the Truman doctrine in 1947 to contain Communism, and initiated the Marshall Plan to rebuild Europe. He oversaw the creation of NATO in 1949. He sent US troops to fight North Korea in the Korean War between 1950 and 1953. US and UN forces were thrown back by Chinese military intervention, and the war became a stalemate during his Presidency. Truman started racial integration in the military and federal agencies.

Myth debunked: Harry Truman used the phrase "the buck stops here," but he didn't originate it.

Facts: Harry Truman's middle name was plain "S." His business ventures (including running a sewing supply shop) were not particularly successful. When he became President, Truman was in the dark about WWII matters, as FDR had not kept him informed. Truman survived an assassination attempt in 1950; he wasn't harmed, but a guard died in the line of duty. Truman had two dogs.

34. Dwight D. Eisenhower (1890–1969)
Party: Republican
Terms: 1953–1961 (two terms)

Dwight D. Eisenhower was an Army General in WWII prior to becoming President. He was the first president whose term was limited by the 22nd Amendment. He threatened the use of nuclear weapons in Korea, ordered coups in Iran and Guatemala, strongly helped France in the beginning of the Vietnam War (supporting South Vietnam), established NASA, sent troops to Lebanon to prop up a friendly regime there, coined the term "military–industrial complex," opposed Joseph McCarthy, and launched the Interstate Highway system. He also created ARPA, the Advanced Research Projects Agency, which later became known as DARPA (Defense Advanced Research Projects Agency).

Myth debunked: Eisenhower was actually born David Dwight Eisenhower, not "Dwight D."

Facts: Eisenhower's nickname was Ike and the slogan "I Like Ike" made him something of a legend. (Actually, he was "Little Ike" and his brother, Edgar, was "Big Ike.") Eisenhower was a highly regarded five star general, but he never actually fought in combat. Eisenhower loved to paint and created some two hundred paintings in his lifetime. He had a dog and a parakeet, but he despised cats to such an extent he shot any that ventured near his home.

35. John F. Kennedy (1917–1963)
Party: Democrat
Term: 1961–1963 (one term, assassinated while in office)

John F. Kennedy

John F. Kennedy (JFK) was a Navy hero who served in the US House of Representatives and the US Senate prior to becoming President. He is the only Roman Catholic President to date and the first President born in the twentieth century. He rapidly increased American involvement in Vietnam, sending eighteen times as many advisors there as Eisenhower did. His attempt to overthrow Fidel Castro, the leader of Cuba, failed and became known as the Bay of Pigs. JFK oversaw the Cuban Missile Crisis. He was assassinated in 1963 by Lee Harvey Oswald during his first term, becoming the fourth and most recent President to have been assassinated while in office.

Myth debunked: At last, one Kennedy/Lincoln coincidence has been proven untrue! Did Lincoln have a secretary named Kennedy and did Kennedy have a secretary named

Lincoln? No. Kennedy's secretary was Evelyn Lincoln, but Lincoln's secretaries were John Hay and John G. Nicolay—neither a Kennedy.

Facts: JFK is the only President to have won a Pulitzer Prize; it was earned for his book, *Profiles in Courage.* There are myriad odd coincidences between JFK and Abraham Lincoln: both had successor Vice Presidents named Johnson; both were shot in the back of the head with their wives present; both assassins, Booth and Oswald, were killed before facing a trial; and on and on. Freaky Friday: All four Presidents who were shot to death (Kennedy, McKinley, Garfield, and Lincoln) were murdered on a Friday. Kennedy was said to have referred to his penis as "JJ."

It is well known JFK was a notorious philanderer, and these beautiful ladies were among his numerous reported conquests: actresses Marlene Dietrich, Marilyn Monroe, Angie Dickinson, and Gene Tierney; stripper Blaze Starr; Swedish socialite Gunilla Von Post; White House intern Mimi Alford; German prostitute Ellen Rometsch; Frank Sinatra's ex-lover Judith Campbell Exner; socialite/old flame Mary Pinchot Meyer; White House secretaries "Fiddle" and "Faddle"; and Jackie's press secretary, Pamela Turnure.

Speaking of First Lady Kennedy, who later became Jackie Kennedy Onnasis, when did she find time alone with her husband to have four children (Caroline, JFK Jr., Patrick, and Arabella)? The Kennedy family had a menagerie of dogs, cats, birds, ponies, horses, and a rabbit named Zsa Zsa. Pushinka, the puppy of space dog Strelka, was gifted to JFK by Soviet Premier Khrushchev.

36. Lyndon B. Johnson (1908-1973)

Party: Democrat

Terms: 1963-1969 (two terms, succeeded Kennedy after his assassination)

Lyndon B. Johnson, known simply as LBJ, was a United States Representative and the Majority Leader in the United States Senate prior to serving as Vice President under JFK and succeeding him to the office after his assassination. LBJ signed several civil rights bills banning racial discrimination and the Voting Rights Act, which blocked certain requirements Southern states had used to disenfranchise black voters. LBJ was passionate about education and put forth both the Elementary and Secondary Education Act and Higher Education Act. He escalated American involvement in Vietnam even further than JFK. He was granted power by Congress to use military force in Southeast Asia without having to ask for an official declaration of war. He increased the number of military personnel in Vietnam from 16,000 advisors in 1963 to 550,000 troops in 1968. As the Vietnam War became increasingly unpopular and crime rates began to rise at home, Johnson's popularity fell and he decided not to run for a full second term.

Myth debunked: LBJ did not originate the phrase "We shall overcome," but instead borrowed it from African American leaders for his March 15, 1965 speech regarding racial violence in Selma, Alabama.

Facts: LBJ's record is a mixed bag: He accomplished a great deal for civil rights and education, but he also entangled the US deeper in the Vietnam War and couldn't soothe social unrest within the country. A large man at six foot three (though not as tall as Lincoln), he used his size to intimidate people. He was also known for being uncouth, having a penchant for swearing and belching in people's faces. On one occasion, he peed on a Secret Service man. Johnson referred to his Johnson as, well, "Jumbo" and was known to proudly display it to others in the men's bathroom. He had several dogs, including beagles named Him and Her and a mongrel named Yuki. He also had hamsters and lovebirds.

37. Richard Nixon (1913-1994)
Party: Republican
Terms: 1969–1974, (two terms, resigned before second term ended)

Richard Nixon

Richard Milhous Nixon was an attorney and Senator prior to becoming Vice President alongside President Eisenhower. He lost his first Presidential bid to JFK, but years later defeated Hubert Humphrey to become number 37. As President, Nixon opened diplomatic relations with Communist China for the first time, enforced desegregation of southern schools, and oversaw the Apollo 11 Moon landing. He was incredibly popular during his first term and won his second term by a landslide. Although Nixon declared the Vietnam War was "ending" in 1969, it has now become known that he privately continued it for political gain (and it did not officially end until 1975). His second term also saw the Arab oil embargo, gasoline rationing, and the infamous Watergate scandal. This last scandal and its cover-up destroyed his Presidency. Facing certain impeachment and removal from office, he voluntarily resigned from office in 1974, thereby becoming the only US President to ever do so. He was pardoned by his successor, President Gerald Ford.

Myth debunked: Who won the first televised Presidential debate on September 26, 1960? Myth has it that Kennedy won according to viewers who saw it on TV, whereas Nixon won it according to radio listeners. There is no real evidence to support this claim: The one survey done was based on 2,100 respondents, only 282 of whom listened to the debate on the radio.

Facts: Many of Nixon's early accomplishments as President have been buried by his scandals and mocked persona. Nixon was known as "Trickie Dickie" for a variety of reasons, but primarily because of his dirty political campaign tactics. He used wiretapping methods against friends and foes alike. He kept his own tapes—many of which were self-incriminating and/or captured him negatively—because he thought they would later be worth a great deal of money. Nixon was particularly paranoid about certain influential rock and roll figures—notably former Beatle John Lennon—and had the FBI post surveillance on him. Nixon had several dogs.

38. Gerald Ford (1913-2006)
Party: Republican
Term: 1974-1977 (one term, succeeded Nixon after his resignation)

Gerald Ford, born Leslie Lynch King, Jr., was a Michigan Representative prior to becoming Vice President under

Nixon and succeeded to the office after his resignation. One of his first acts was to pardon the former President. Interestingly, Ford is the only person in U.S. history to have served as both Vice President and President without having been elected to either office. The Vietnam War officially ended nine months into his Presidency. He presided over the worst economy in the four decades since the Great Depression with rising inflation and a Recession. He lost his bid for re-election.

Myth debunked: Some people believe that Ford's pardon of Nixon helped "heal the nation." The fact is, the move caused Ford's ratings to take a nosedive overnight from which he never truly recovered.

Facts: Gerald R. Ford International Airport in Grand Rapids, MI was named after him. As a young man, Ford was quite a good football player and had offers to play for the Detroit Lions and the Green Bay Packers. Ford was on the Warren Commission, which investigated the assassination of JFK. Chevy Chase, the comedian who spoofed Ford as a klutz on *Saturday Night Live*, liked the President and later became his friend. Ford had several dogs and a Siamese cat named Shan. Misty, a puppy, was born while Ford lived in the White House.

39. Jimmy Carter (1924–alive as of this writing)
Party: Democrat
Term: 1977–1981 (one term)

Jimmy Carter was Governor of Georgia prior to becoming President number 39. On his second day in office he pardoned all evaders of the Vietnam War drafts. He returned the Panama Canal Zone to Panama and oversaw the beginning of the Iran hostage crisis. He was President during the Three Mile Island nuclear accident and the

Soviet invasion of Afghanistan. As a response to the latter, he led the 1980 boycott of the Olympics in Moscow. Carter facilitated peace between Israel and Egypt at the Camp David Accords. His popularity eroded greatly by the next election and he lost in a landslide to Ronald Reagan in 1980.

Myth debunked: Jimmy Carter's brother, Billy, was something of an embarrassment to the President. For one thing, he became a registered agent of Libya. For another, he was known to make public scenes, such as when he urinated on an airport runway. His product, Billy Beer, became something of a hoax. Although Billy frequently stated his beer was "delicious," he often deflated his own marketing by getting drunk and saying he preferred Pabst Blue Ribbon. The beer was a total flop.

Facts: : Carter was not a popular President, as he failed to recover American hostages from Iran and protested Soviet expansion by boycotting the Olympics. During his term, interest rates and unemployment were high and America faced a painful energy crisis with gas rationing and long lines at the pump. No one has ever doubted Carter is a "good man," as his relentless charitable work on a number of humanitarian issues—AIDS, conservation, environment, human rights, education, rights, to name a few—since his Presidency has been significant. Carter had two dogs.

40. Ronald Reagan (1911–2004)

Party: Republican
Terms: 1981–1989 (two terms)

Ronald Reagan

Ronald Reagan was a Hollywood actor and the Governor of California prior to becoming President number 40. At age sixty-nine he became the oldest elected President in US history (until Donald Trump). Reagan advocated for supply-side economic policies, reduced taxes, escalated the War on Drugs, reduced inflation from 12.5 percent to 4.4 percent, and oversaw the end of the Cold War. He also led the US bombing of Libya. Six months after his second term, the world saw the collapse of the Berlin Wall. On March 30, 1981, he survived an assassination attempt in which he was shot by John Hinckley, Jr.

Myth debunked: Was Reagan a "bad actor"? Many of the films he appeared in were bad (*Bedtime for Bonzo*, anyone?), but Reagan himself wasn't quite so awful in films such as *Knute Rockne, All American* or *King's Row.* He was a brilliant orator, more so than a "good" actor, and had a unique ability to win over audiences and make people laugh.

Facts: Reagan's nicknames included "the Gipper," "Dutch," "the Great Communicator," and "The Teflon President." Sixteen million jobs were created under Reagan's watch. He strengthened America's military might with a "Peace through strength" philosophy. His Star Wars Strategic Defense Initiative faced opposition, but over time the technology he envisioned has to some extent come to pass. Reagan officially announced in 1994 that he had Alzheimer's disease, which many people assert caused his memory lapses during his second term as President. His cause of death was pneumonia resulting from the Alzheimer's. He had many dogs and horses.

41. George H.W. Bush (1924-still alive as of this writing)

Party: Republican
Term: 1989-1993 (one term)

George Herbert Walker Bush was a Representative of the 7th District in Texas, US Ambassador to the United Nations, Director of the CIA, and Vice President under Reagan prior to being elected President. Bush, the last President to have served in WWII, was a pilot who survived being shot down by the Japanese. As President, he conducted military operations in Panama and oversaw the First Gulf War against Saddam Hussein's Iraq. The Berlin Wall fell in 1989 early into his term, and the Soviet Union collapsed only two years later. He pledged during his campaign to not raise taxes—but his popularity plunged when he went against his word and raised them. He is the last President to serve only one term.

Myth debunked: It became popularized that Bush was so out of touch that he didn't know what a scanner was at a supermarket checkout. This was the result of some manipulation by the press.

Facts: As of this writing, Bush is the oldest living President at ninety-three years of age. He and his wife had six children (George W., Jeb, Neil, Dorothy, Marvin, and Robin). Robin Bush died from leukemia as a child. Only George W. and Jeb entered politics. George Bush played first base for the Yale baseball team and was team captain in 1948. Bush was not a popular President and is best remembered for having raised taxes and for puking on the lap of Japanese Prime Minister Kiichi Miyazawa. Bush had a dog named Millie who had puppies in the White House.

42. Bill Clinton (1946-still alive as of this writing)

Party: Democrat
Terms: 1993-2001 (two terms)

Bill Clinton

Bill Clinton was Arkansas Attorney General and Governor of Arkansas prior to becoming President number 42. He was the first President from the Baby-Boomer generation. He signed NAFTA into law and passed welfare reform. Clinton ordered US Military intervention in the Bosnia and Kosovo wars against Serbia, and participated in the 2000 Camp David Summit to help out peace between Israel and Palestine. In 1998 Clinton became the second President to be impeached because had sexual encounters while in office with White House intern Monica Lewinsky, and then perjured himself by lying about it. He was acquitted by the Senate in 1999 and served out a full second term. Clinton left office with the highest approval rating of any President since WWII.

Myth debunked: Some pretty crazy tales have been told about Bill Clinton, including unsubstantiated claims that there is a "body count" of people he had killed— including Whitewater partner James McDougal, who died of a heart attack.

Facts: Among Bill Clinton's numerous nicknames: "Slick Willie," "Bubba," and "Compromiser in Chief." Bill Clinton allegedly had consensual and non-consensual sexual relations with a number of women. Among the alleged consensual: Monica Lewinsky, Gennifer Flowers, Dolly Kyle Browning, and Sally Perdue. Among the alleged non-consensual: Juanita Broaddrick, Paula Jones, and Kathleen Wiley. The allegations and scandals scar Clinton's accomplishments as President: 22 million jobs created; highest home ownership in history; lowest unemployment in thirty years; improved education standards and school connections to the Internet; lowest crime rate in twenty-six years; highest income levels and lowest poverty levels in years; lowest teen births in sixty years; and $360 billion paid off the national debt. His wife, Hillary Clinton, became Secretary of State and lost her Presidential bid to Donald Trump (despite winning the popular vote). Bill and Hillary's daughter, Chelsea, was an NBC news correspondent and currently works for the Clinton Foundation and Clinton Global Initiative. While Bill Clinton was President, Chelsea had a famous cat named Socks and the family had a Lab named Buddy.

43. George W. Bush (1946-still alive as of this writing)
Party: Republican
Terms: 2001-2009 (two terms)

George W. Bush, the son of George H. W. Bush, was the Governor of Texas, an oil company owner, and Major League Baseball team owner (the Texas Rangers) prior to becoming President. He became the fourth President to have been elected while receiving fewer popular votes than his opponent (Al Gore). The 9/11 terrorist attacks occurred only eight months into the Bush Presidency. Bush launched the War on Terror, which included wars in Afghanistan and Iraq. He signed into law tax cuts, the Patriot Act, and No Child Left Behind. He received criticism for the real motivations behind the Iraq War—no weapons of mass destruction were ever discovered—and lack of proper response on Hurricane Katrina. In December 2007, under his watch, the US entered the Recession: the worst financial crisis since the Great Depression. Bush received significant criticism for not having done enough to end the Recession.

Myth debunked: G.W. liked to present the image of being a cowboy, but he grew up mostly in New Haven, CT and had an Ivy League education at Yale University and Harvard Business School.

Facts: G.W. has been nicknamed "Dubya" and "Junior." One of his lesser moments was being captured on film sitting in a school classroom for over seven minutes after having been told about the 9/11 attacks. Since leaving office, G.W. has become a critically praised painter. His brother Jeb, the former Governor of California, was expected by many to also someday become President—but to date this has not occurred. G.W.'s wife, Laura, had the highest approval rating of any First Lady in history. G.W. Bush had several dogs, a cat, and a cow named Ofelia (at his ranch).

44. Barack Obama (1961-still alive as of this writing)
Party: Democrat
Terms: 2009-2017 (two terms)

Barack Obama

Barack Obama was an Illinois Senator prior to becoming President number 44. He was the first African American to become President of the US, as well as the first born outside the Continental US. (He was born in Hawaii.) Obama ended U.S. military involvement in Iraq, increased troop levels in Afghanistan, ordered military involvement in Libya against Gaddafi, and ordered the military operation that resulted in the death of Al Qaeda terrorist leader Osama Bin Laden. Obama oversaw the striking down of same-sex marriage bans, ordered the restart of military involvement in Iraq, promoted the 2015 Paris Agreement on global climate change, brokered a nuclear deal with Iran, and normalized US relations with Cuba. President Obama passed the controversial Affordable Care Act (now better known as Obamacare), rescued the American economy from the Recession, and passed Wall Street reform.

Myth debunked: There are too many to mention here, but these are the most important: 1. He is a Christian and never was a Muslim (or a terrorist). 2. He was born an American citizen (in Hawaii), contrary to ludicrous Birther claims by political opponents, such as Donald Trump.

Facts: Obama's achievements are undeniable given the Recession he faced on entering the Presidency. He created 11.3 million jobs and the Dow rose 140 percent during his two terms. Unlike most other Presidents, Obama did not have any sexual affairs and was free of major scandals. Obama won the Nobel Peace Prize nine months after his inauguration. On the flip side, many people feel that Obama strained relations with Israel—one of the country's closest allies. Obama loves playing basketball. His wife, Michelle Obama, is an accomplished attorney who had a high approval rating as First Lady. The Obamas had two dogs at different times named Bo and Sunny.

45. Donald J. Trump (1946-still alive as of this writing)
Party: Republican
Term: 2017-Present (still in first term as of this writing)

What can one say about number 45 that won't stir intense emotions? Trump was a real estate mogul and investor, hotelier, clothing producer, reality show host, and tabloid mainstay prior to becoming President of the United States. Trump is the only President in history to have had zero political or military experience. As of this writing early on in the Presidency, Trump's first term has been marred by scandals, controversies, and setbacks that have besotted his agenda: investigations into his campaign's collusion with Russia hacking and his obstruction of justice; the firing of FBI director James Comey; failure to repeal or replace Obamacare; firings and in-fighting within his administration and staff; failure to enact a Muslim ban; pulling the US out of the Paris Agreement on climate change; and receiving lack of support for building a border Wall with Mexico (and having them pay for it). On a positive note for Trump's party, he successfully nominated Neil Gorsuch to the Supreme Court. Unscripted, he threatened "fire and fury" against North Korea if they continued nuclear threats. In August 2017, Trump stirred major controversy by failing to condemn white supremacists who held a rally in Charlottesville, which led to the death of counter-protestor Heather Heyer. *Whew*, what will be next?

Myth debunked: Trump has stated that he wants business to remain in America and have manufacturing moved back to this country. His claims that his products were made in America are false; his ties, for example, were produced in China.

Facts: Donald Trump has been called many things, the majority of which are not favorable. Let's leave it at "The Twitter President," since he is the first President to use this form of social interaction as his main form of communication. As President, Trump has been an equal opportunity basher, attacking and blaming political rivals (Hillary Clinton and Barack Obama) as much as members of his own party (Jeff Sessions, John McCain, and Mitch McConnell). He has also entered Twitter wars with celebrities Rosie O'Donnell, Mika Brzezinski, Arnold Schwarzenegger, Kathy Griffin, and myriad others. Meanwhile, he has lavished praise on Russian President Vladimir Putin. Trump is well known as a fan of Fox News and Breitbart as his primary sources of information, referring to most other news organizations as "fake news." Trump has had three wives and is currently married to Melania Trump, who was born in Slovenia. As a businessman, Trump has filed for bankruptcy four times and, as of this writing, has refused to disclose his taxes which he claims are under audit. (There is no evidence to support this fact.) Trump's daughter (Ivanka) and son-in-law (Jared Kushner) are in his administration. Trump loves fast food and golf. He has no pets.

HOW MUCH DO YOU KNOW ABOUT PRESIDENTS?

1. Who are the only Presidents to have had no pets?

2. Who was the only single President in his lifetime?

3. Which President had the most wives?

4. Were George Washington's teeth made of wood?

5. What genetic disease did Lincoln likely have?

CONCLUSION

MISCELLANEOUS THOUGHTS AND FACTS

Facts are meaningless. You could use facts to prove anything that's even remotely true! Facts shmacts.

—Homer Simpson, character on *The Simpsons*

How do I conclude a book of this intentionally random nature?

In a video, I can simply roll credits, cut away, fade out, or just stop. In a book, usually the author likes to summarize things and put things in perspective. No thank you—I would much rather not do that.

Instead of diving deep into exploring subjects as I did in the previous chapters, I am going to go the opposite route and give you a bunch of nuggets/sound bytes to chew on (including more about the Earl of Sandwich). I think this is only fair, as you are probably exhausted by now from reading so much detail about things like credit, antipodes, Vikings, and Presidents.

You Can't Have Enough Sandwiches

The life of the 4th Earl of Sandwich (mentioned in Chapter Ten) was perhaps even more controversial than his invention. When his wife went insane, he took on a teenage mistress named Martha Ray. A newly ordained priest named James Hackilometersan fell in love with Martha while the Earl was posted in Ireland. When Hackilometersan suspected her of being with yet another man, he shot her. Reverend Hackilometersan was tried and executed for the crime. The Earl of Sandwich was despondent over his lover's death, but at least he had two slices of bread and salty meat to serve as his comfort food.

What Is the Easiest to Burn Calories?

They say that just moving away from your desk several times a day and going for sporadic walks can help you burn calories. Here are some not-so-obvious, easy ways to burn calories: laughing for ten minutes (40 calories), rising from the couch thirty-three times to change the channel (100 calories), banging your head against a wall (150 calories per hour; okay, this might not be so easy), and having sex (90-120 calories per hour; not easy if you don't have a partner).

How Many Starbucks Are There?

As of this writing, there are 24,000 Starbucks stores around the world spread out over seventy countries; 7,559 of these Starbucks stores are in the United States. It is projected that Starbucks will surpass McDonald's in revenue by 2025. The farthest location away from a Starbucks in the US is in Circle, Montana, which is some 192 miles away from a Starbucks.

The average Starbucks consumer spends a fortune on coffee each year. If this same average customer were to stop buying a tall cup of coffee for one year, he or she would have enough to purchase a new iPhone.

Coffee Cup

Can Cats See in the Dark?

Yes—cats have remarkable eyes and only require about one sixth of the light of humans in order to see. Why? Because they have a large amount of rods in their retinas that are sensitive to dim light. Cats cannot see in total darkness, however. They are also not totally color blind, as was previously believed; they can make out some colors, but can't discern green from red.

Which Classic Comedy Teams Were Real Brothers?

The Marx Brothers were a comedy team made up of real life brothers: Groucho (Julius), Harpo (Adolph), Chico (Leonard), Zeppo (Herbert), and Gummo (Milton).

The Ritz Brothers were also real brothers: Al, Jimmy, and Harry. (A fourth, George, was their manager; and they had a sister, Gertrude.)

The three Stooges, naturally, were a bit more confusing. Moses, Jerome, and Samuel Horowitz were indeed brothers and, respectively, became famously known as Moe, Curly, and Shemp Howard. However, Shemp was not part of the original "famed" trio with the other brothers, which included non-brother Larry Fine (Larry Feinberg) instead. Later replacements for Curly—Joe Besser and Joe DeRita (a.k.a. Curly Joe)—were unrelated to the Howards (or was it Horowitzes?).

How Much Garbage Do We Have?

A ton! Each year, humans toss out 2.12 billion tons of garbage. It is estimated that 99 percent of what is purchased is thrown away within six months. Roughly speaking, we need about two planets to contain all of the world's garbage. Meanwhile, humans have created about nine billion tons of plastic since the 1950s; even with modern recycling efforts, only 9 percent is currently being recycled.

Can You Get Drunk from Water?

Yes, even too much of a good thing such as water can be bad—but not in the way you think. Too much water intake all at once can cause a fatal situation known as *water intoxication.* Cases have been cited among athletes who died from drinking too much while replenishing fluids or trying to alleviate muscle cramps.

When a person drinks too much water, the blood becomes dangerously diluted of salts. This leads to a state known as *hyponatremia*; severe cases can cause water intoxication.

It only takes six liters or 1.6 gallons of water at one time to drown a person weighing 165 pounds. That isn't much when one considers that we are encouraged to drink a lot of water to stay healthy (two liters or a half gallon per day).

Imbibe safely—but at least you can drink water and drive.

Who Was the Real "Fifth Beatle"?

Many have laid claim to this title, but no one outside John, Paul, George, and Ringo were ever officially called a "Beatle." These are the main candidates for who "could" have been considered a Fifth Beatle:

- Pete Best: drummer of The Beatles prior to Ringo Starr

- Stuart Sutcliffe: talented artist friend of John who fumbled playing bass with the band before they made records

- Tony Sheridan: singer who hired the young Beatles as his backup band ("the Beat Boys") around 1961

- Andy White: session drummer who played on "Love Me Do" before producer George Martin was comfortable with Ringo Starr on drums

- Jimmy Nicol: drummer who filled in on tour in 1964 when Ringo had his tonsils removed

- Murray the K: a DJ who helped popularize The Beatles in America and actually became dubbed "the Fifth Beatle" (without their technical consultation/approval)

- Brian Epstein: Beatles manager

- Eric Clapton: guitarist extraordinaire of The Yardbirds, Cream, Derek and the Dominoes, etc., who played (uncredited) guitar on The Beatles song "While My Guitar Gently Weeps," written by George Harrison

- Billy Preston: gifted keyboardist and composer who played piano on "Get Back" and other songs on the *Let It Be* sessions. Preston is the only artist credited with The Beatles for his contributions ("The Beatles with Billy Preston" on "Get Back")

- George Martin: The Beatles brilliant producer, whose innovative musical contributions cannot be underscored

- Neil Aspinall: Road manager and Beatles friend

- Derek Taylor: Beatles press officer

- Yoko Ono: John's lover and then wife, who visited recording sessions and sang on "The Continuing Story of Bungalow Bill."

So, who would our pick be for Fifth Beatle? The Beatles themselves eschewed the moniker the "Fifth Beatle," so outside of Murray the K it's doubtful anyone else could credibly trumpet having that honor. But if we absolutely had to choose someone...

Let's start by the process of elimination. Murray the K was a disc jockey who promoted The Beatles on radio. The Beatles liked him and appeared on air with him, but really the title was nothing more than shtick on Murray's part. He had nothing to do with the band except for radio airplay.

What about George Martin, The Beatles' maestro producer? Yes, he happened to go far above and beyond in their music making and innovation—and even played an instrument now and then—but that doesn't make him a band member. For one thing, he didn't write or sing any of their songs. Could you have seen him on stage with long hair performing with the group? Smoking pot and taking LSD? I don't think so.

Session musicians, fill-ins, roadies, and other related studio personnel in their inner circle are also excluded. They were doing their jobs.

What about a Beatle wife, such as Yoko? Err—no thanks. Paul, George, and Ringo would never have accepted her as a band member—and millions of fans would have my head.

That really boils things down to Eric Clapton and Billy Preston, who were specifically invited to play on records and made significant creative contributions to the music. Of the two, I would omit Clapton and go with Preston as Fifth Beatle because he was involved in much of the *Let It Be* sessions, played live on the rooftop alongside The Beatles, created that super cool piano groove on "Get Back," and was given a shared "with" credit on a Beatles record. Such shared credit hadn't really occurred except with Tony Sheridan years earlier, and even then, it was The Beatles who were the backing band and second fiddle to Sheridan. On top of all that, John Lennon once suggested that Preston be asked to join the group.

Sorry, God—I mean, Mr. Clapton!

All We Are Saying Is—Give Silver a Chance

Everybody's talking about gold—gold, gold, gold. There are around 178 words that have *gold* in it (*goldfish*, *golden*, *goldeneye*, you get the idea…) but only about fifty-one that contain the word *silver* (*quicksilver*, *silverware*, *silversmith*, you get the idea).

I even devoted a whole chapter in this book to gold, so I admit a bias myself. Why does silver pale so much in comparison to gold?

Silver is a valuable precious metal that, like gold, is made into jewelry. It is an excellent conductor of electricity and can be molded into shiny coins. Silver has many unusual uses, including medical treatments (silver nitrate is a wart remover), deodorant, and batteries.

The main reason it's not held in the same high regard as gold is that it's simply not as rare. There also was never a Bond villain named Silverfinger.

TRIVIA ANSWERS

Chapter One:

1. Lebanon, Egypt, Jordan, and Syria border Israel.

2. The US bought California from Mexico.

3. Italy became known as a unified country in 1851.

4. China built the Great Wall to protect against invaders, such as the Mongols.

5. Yes, Korea was once unified. The Japanese had control of the country and annexed it in 1910. After Japan was defeated in World War II, the territory was divided into North and South Korea.

Chapter Two:

1. The 1920 British Empire was the world's largest. The Empire owned nearly 24 percent of the world's territory.

2. Genghis Khan ruled over Mongolia.

3. The Solomonic Dynasty in Ethiopia, which ruled for 2,900 years, is believed to be the longest running empire in history. Some believe they were so named "Solomonic" because they descended from Jewish King Solomon.

4. No, it's a myth that Napoleon Bonaparte was short. He was likely around 5'7", which makes him average height for a man in his era.

5. Empress Wu Zetian of China was a concubine before she wed Emperor Taizong. She became empress consort, empress dowager, and empress regnant and ruled China for many years during the Zhou and Tang dynasties.

Chapter Three:

1. Indonesia is the nearest country to Australia.

2. Mount Chimborazo is closest to the equator.

3. The two highest-flying birds: Ruppell's griffon vulture (37,000 feet, the height of a commercial airplane) and the bar-headed goose (nearly 28,000 feet).

4. It would take a person approximately 225 million years to walk a light year.

5. The Earth is closest to the sun during a period known as perihelion when it comes within 147.5 million kilometers.

Chapter Four:

1. Yes, Kiribati is a country. It is an island located in the Central Pacific Ocean and has a population just over 100,000.

2. No, Klaatu is not (and never was) a country. Klaatu is the name of a 1970's progressive rock band inspired by the name of the alien character in the film *The Day the Earth Stood Still*.

3. France has the most time zones with twelve.

4. Actor and comedian Sacha Baron Cohen is British. He was born in Hammersmith, London.

Chapter Five:

1. Pretty much every country has been in some conflict or other over the years. Only two countries can lay claim to having avoided war the longest among those countries currently in existence. The first is Greenland, which doesn't have a military but has some defenses provided by Denmark. The second is Switzerland, whose last real war engagement dates all the way back to 1847 and their civil war, known as the Sonderbund War.

2. Abhazia, located south of Russia on the eastern coast of the Black Sea, is the only real "country" among the choices provided. Technically, it is only a "partially recognized state" with areas being claimed by Georgia. The population of Abhazia is around 243,000. Druidia, by the way, is a planet in the Mel Brooks film *Spaceballs*.

3. Kataan is a fictional planet referenced in the *Star Trek Next Generation* series. Fans will recognize it from one of the show's finest episodes, "The Inner Light."

4. Scarlett Johansson is the only actor from the list who was born in the US—Manhattan, to be precise.

5. The Sahara Desert is ginormous (nearly 3.6 million square miles, almost the size of China) and covers much of the North African continent and eleven recognized countries: Algeria, Chad, Egypt, Libya, Mali, Mauritania, Morocco, Niger, Sudan, Tunisia, Western Sahara.

Chapter Six:

1. John F. Kennedy was the first US President to be accompanied by the nuclear football.

2. The Secretary of the Department of the Interior is a member of the President's cabinet who leads the Department of the Interior. Essentially, this means overseeing lands and resources that are run by the government, such as the US national parks.

3. Peter Sellers plays three roles in Stanley Kubrick's *Dr. Strangelove*: British officer Lionel Mandrake; US President Merkin Muffley; and ex-Nazi nuclear expert Dr. Strangelove. Most people are unaware that he was cast in a fourth role, Texan Major T.J. Kong. At first, Sellers was reluctant to play the role of Major Kong due to the challenging Texan accent. He caved and agreed to take it on once he received some coaching on Texan drawl from screenwriter Terry Southern himself. However, Sellers suffered an ankle injury, which made it impossible for him to be filmed in the airplane cockpit, where Major Kong's character appears for the entirety of the film. He was replaced by Slim Pickens and the rest is history (or the *end* of history...*yeehaw!*).

4. No President has owned an NFL football team. However, George W. Bush headed the investment team that purchased the Texas Rangers Major League Baseball team in 1989.

5. Yes, Putin does indeed have his own version of a nuclear football—only it's not referred to as a "football." The Russian nuclear briefcase is called a *cheget*. In 1995 the *cheget* was put on readiness alert

by Boris Yeltsin when Russia believed a rocket fired by Norwegian and American scientists was a nuclear threat. It was the only time in history the briefcase was used. Fortunately, the threat ended when the Norwegian rocket changed course and the nuclear alert was turned off.

Chapter Seven:

1. Karl Gerhart Fröbe portrayed the villainous *Goldfinger*. Fröbe had been a German and member of the Nazi party during World War II. *Goldfinger* was banned in Israel as a result—until it was proven that Fröbe helped two Jews hide from other Nazis, and he was vindicated.

2. The most expensive gold gadget is the Stuart Hughes Gold and Black Diamond iPhone 5, which is valued at $15 million USD.

3. The highest percentage of gold has come from the Witwatersrand Basin in South Africa. Nearly 40 percent of all gold mined in the last century and a quarter has come from this area.

4. President Richard Nixon stopped the gold standard in the US in 1971.

5. By far, the United States has the largest gold reserve in the world with 8,133.5 tonnes. This is significantly more than the combined amount of the next two countries—Germany and Italy.

Chapter Eight:

1. Industrial and Commercial Bank of China is the largest in the world with nearly $3.5 billion in assets.

2. J.P. Morgan and Chase is the largest bank in the United States with assets of $2.5 billion.

3. The five countries with zero debt: Macao, British Virgin Islands, Brunei, Liechtenstein, and Palau.

4. The top five countries with the most debt (in order): the United States, the United Kingdom, France, Germany, and the Netherlands.

5. The world's largest credit card company is Visa with 323 million cardholders.

Chapter Nine:

1. It is uncertain where "Why did the chicken cross the road?" originated, but the first printed sign of it appeared in *The Knickerbocker* literary magazine in 1847.

2. The most traveled road in the United States is I-405 in CA, which stretches from Long Beach to Santa Ana. Some 374,000 vehicles travel on it each day.

3. The most common street name—drum roll, please—is *not* First Street (which is third). Number one is actually *Second* Street. Main Street comes in seventh.

4. The first recorded auto accident involving a gasoline-powered car occurred in Ohio City, Ohio in 1891 when engineer James Lambert drove one of his creations into a hitching post. Lambert and his passenger suffered only minor injuries.

5. According to a number of sources (including Ranker. com as of this writing), Miami has the most road rage followed by New York City.

Chapter Ten:

1. The deepest human-made hole is the Kola Superdeep Borehole in the Kola Peninsula, which goes down 7.5 miles. Scientists had to stop digging due to the scorching 356 degrees Fahrenheit temperature.

2. The Bingham County Mine in Utah begun in 1906 is the widest human-made hole at 2.5 miles wide and three quarters of a mile deep. It continues to be the world's largest copper mine.

3. Dragon Hole, a sinkhole located in the South China Sea, is the largest natural hole on record at 300.89 meters (987.2 feet) deep.

4. A sandwich was *sort of* eaten in space...which we'll count as a *yes*. In 1965, pilot John Young smuggled a corned beef sandwich onto the Gemini 3, one of the early test flights for the moon voyage. The sandwich was exposed for about ten seconds when crumbs began to break apart and cause a potential hazard. Sandwiches were banned thereafter and only allowed as bite-sized cubes. In 1981, Young commanded a space mission on which he was able to eat a bite-sized corned beef sandwich.

5. The answer is (c) there is no such synonym for *antipode*. One would be hard-pressed to come up with an opposite word for the opposite (e.g., antipode), which would be a positive. As for the other answers: *Posipode* and *podpos* aren't words at all, while a megapode is a chicken-like bird that can be found in the Australasia region.

Chapter Eleven:

1. Andrew Johnson tended to mice, so really the only President who never had a pet of any kind is Donald Trump.

2. James Buchanan was the only President who was single throughout his lifetime.

3. Donald Trump is the President who had the most wives with three. Only one prior President ever had one divorce—Ronald Reagan.

4. George Washington's teeth were not made of wood. They were likely made (at different times) of human teeth, cow teeth, horse teeth, ivory, and various metals.

5. Lincoln is now believed to have had Marfan syndrome, a connective tissue disease characterized by great height, as well as long legs, arms, fingers, and toes. The disease has been associated with scoliosis and various heart issues.

NOTES

Antipode Source (https://en.wikipedia.org/wiki/Antipodes)

SADR Source (https://en.wikipedia.org/wiki/Sahrawi_Arab_Democratic_Republic)

Map of Lesotho (Peter Hermes Furian, Shutterstock.com)

Map of Vatican City (Peter Hermes Furian, Shutterstock.com)

Location of San Marino (David Petrik, Shutterstock.com)

Korean DMZ, Panmunjom (JNEZAM, Shutterstock.com)

The Roman Empire 117 AD (Peter Hermes Furian, Shutterstock.com)

King Cnut's Empire

German Empire in 1914

Modern Germany (boreala, Shutterstock.com)

Point Nemo (Alex Wolf, Shutterstock.com)

Kosovo (Marco Rosales, Shutterstock.com)

ROC and PRC (Harvepino, Shutterstock.com)

Western Sahara (Harvepino, Shutterstock.com)

Moldova (dovla982, Shutterstock.com)

Armenia (Harvepino, Shutterstock.com)

Bir Tawil and the Hala'ib Triangle (Peter Hermes Furian, Shutterstock.com)

The Nuclear Football (Nerthuz, Shutterstock.com)

Gold Bars (Novi Elysa, Shutterstock.com)

Death Road in Bolivia (mezzotint, Shutterstock.com)

James Dalton Highway, Alaska (Bangalore Talkies, Shutterstock.com)

Rudyard, Montana (fishvector, Shutterstock.com)

Kerguelen Islands (Peter Hermes Furian, Shutterstock.com)

George Washington (ra3rn, Shutterstock.com)

Thomas Jefferson (vkilikov, Shutterstock.com)

Dolly Madison on 1980's US postage stamp (angiers, Shutterstock.com)

Andrew Jackson (ra3rn, Shutterstock.com)

James K. Polk (Everett Historical, Shutterstock.com)

George Washington (ra3rn, Shutterstock.com)

Thomas Jefferson (vkilikov. Shutterstock.com)

Dolly Madison on 1980's US postage stamp (angiers, Shutterstock.com)

Andrew Jackson (ra3rn, Shutterstock.com)

James K. Polk (Everett Historical, Shutterstock.com)

Abraham Lincoln (lb0007, Shutterstock.com

James A. Garfield examined by Alexander Graham Bell seeking to locate assassin's bullet with electrical detector, 1881 (Everett Historical, Shutterstock.com)

Grover Cleveland (Everett Historical, Shutterstock.com)

Theodore Roosevelt (BlackA.k.a.liko, Shutterstock.com)

Warren G. Harding (Dawn Hudson, Shutterstock.com)

Herbert Hoover (Dawn Hudson, Shutterstock.com)

Franklin D. Roosevelt (Ron and Joe, Shutterstock.com)

John F. Kennedy (Luc Vernimmen, Shutterstock.com)

Richard M. Nixon (Dawn Hudson, Shutterstock.com)

Ronald Reagan (Dawn Hudson, Shutterstock.com)

Bill Clinton (ArielMartin, Shutterstock.com)

Barack Obama (BlackA.k.a.liko, Shutterstock.com)

Coffee cup (Kaleo, Shutterstock.com) Jacobs, Frank. "Transnistrian Time-Slip," The New York Times, May 22, 2012.

https://opinionator.blogs.nytimes.com/2012/05/22/transnistrian-time-slip/?_r=0

AUTHOR

Joseph Pisenti is the sole creator of *RealLifeLore*, an enormously popular YouTube channel that was founded in February 2016 before he earned his first college degree. Joseph was born in Santa Cruz, California and lives in the Dallas, Texas area. He has completed a Bachelor of Arts degree in International Studies, with a concentration in International Security and Diplomacy and a Minor in Russian from the University of North Texas. He is currently attending the same university and is almost complete with a second Bachelor of Arts Degree in Economics.

As of this writing he is only twenty-three-years old, but he believes this problem will eventually be solved with time.

CPSIA information can be obtained
at www.ICGtesting.com
Printed in the USA
LVHW050737030121
675465LV00003B/3